PLOTMAN TO THE RESCUE

A TROUBLESHOOTING GUIDE TO FIXING YOUR TOUGHEST PLOT PROBLEMS

JAMES SCOTT BELL

COMPENDIUM PRESS

ISBN 10: 0-910355-47-9

ISBN: 13: 978-0-910355-47-6

Published by Compendium Press
Woodland Hills, CA

CONTENTS

THE ORIGIN OF PLOTMAN

LONG, long ago, on the planet Plotto, there lived a king named Story and a queen named Structure. So deep was their love that they knew neither of them alone could rule the planet justly. They needed each other. So did the people.

Thus, together, King Story and Queen Structure ushered Plotto into its golden age.

Naturally, they were thrilled when a royal baby was born.

But alas, an evil villain, Vektor Formless, hatched a plan to blow up the planet. The plan was discovered, but not in time to stop the Formless Doomsday Machine countdown.

With tears in their eyes, King Story and Queen Structure lovingly placed their baby into a little rocket ship and sent him to a distant blue planet.

The rocket came to rest in a field in Kansas. An elderly couple, the Essbees, found the baby and decided to raise him as their own. They named him Jay.

As Jay Essbee grew, he began to understand that his mother was a frustrated writer. She had been working on a novel for years, and it was now being rejected by publishers in the east.

This made his mother sad, and Jay Essbee wanted her to be happy.

One day he went into the study and found his mother's manuscript. He read it all the way through in an hour.

When his mother came in and saw Jay sitting in a chair with her pages on his lap, she was astonished.

"What are you doing with my book, Jay?" she asked.

"I read it, Mother," Jay said.

"But you're only eight years old!"

"And yet I read it and understood it."

Mother Essbee trembled into a chair. "What … did you think?"

"I think there is a germ of a great plot, Mother. But the first act drags, and the main character is not forced through a doorway into a great conflict. Some of the scenes lack tension. The plot meanders in places. There is some definite sagging in the middle."

For a long moment Mother Essbee sat frozen, staring at the boy. Then she cried out, "Father!"

Father Essbee came running into the room.

"Our son," Mother Essbee said, "is a book critic!"

"Not a critic," Jay said. "I can help you fix these things."

"But how?" said Mother Essbee.

"It must be he has powers from his own planet," Father Essbee said.

Over the next few weeks, Jay Essbee worked with his mother on her manuscript. When they were finished, Mother Essbee sent it to an agent in New York. The book sold at auction for a million dollars and then to the movies for another million.

After the movie premiere, Mother and Father Essbee took Jay out for ice cream. Mother Essbee said to her son, "We cannot keep your wonderful gift to ourselves. You must take it to the world. Henceforth, you shall be known as Plotman."

She produced a little costume with a large *P* on the front, and a cape with the same *P*. No one seems to know how the costume grew right along with Jay and still fit him when he was an adult.

But we do know this: Plotman has sworn to uphold plot, story, and the bestselling way!

I'VE GOT NO PLOT!

SO YOU'VE DECIDED you want to write a novel. Lawrence Block, the well-known crime writer, has a suggestion at this point: Take two aspirin, lie down on the sofa, and wait for the feeling to pass.

But what if it doesn't? You really, *really* want to write a novel.

If you're starting from absolute scratch, do some self-evaluation first. Here are the basic questions you must answer:

Why do I want to write a novel?

Go ahead. Write 250 words right now answering that question. I'll wait.

* * *

* * *

* * *

* * *

Welcome back.

Here are some acceptable answers:

- For the love of telling stories.
- Because I've always wanted to, but never took a shot.
- Because I'm compelled to; something inside me won't let me alone until I write a novel.

Unacceptable answers:

- My mom says I'm really good.
- I think it would be neat to be able to say I'm a writer.
- It's an easy way to make money.

Before you move on to the next question, make sure your answer is something that grabs you emotionally. You're going to be putting in a lot of time to become a writer of compelling fiction. You will have lots of opportunities to quit. Unless your heart is invested from the get-go, you will not finish the race.

What kind of fiction do I want to write?

There are two general categories of fiction editors and agents talk about: commercial and literary. There's also a hybrid category they call *up-market*, which is a combination of both.

Commercial fiction always has a strong, plot-centric concept. An example is Thomas Harris's *The Silence of the Lambs*. The concept: *The hunt for a serial killer comes down to a young FBI trainee's battle of wits with a brilliant and dangerous flesh-eating psychiatrist.*

Or *Ambush* by James Patterson and James O. Born: *Only Detective Michael Bennett stands in the way of two lethal cartels fighting for New York City's multi-million-dollar opioid trade. And they know where Bennett, and his family, live.*

Literary fiction, on the other hand, tends toward the character-centric. Thus, *The Shipping News* by Annie Proulx, has the following concept: *A man and his two emotionally disturbed daughters return to their ancestral home in Newfoundland, looking to cobble together new lives.*

Feel the difference? The latter still has a plot. Every novel has a plot.

What kind of fiction do you want to write?

What if you love both?

Then decide what's more important to you: money or adulation. It's not that you can't get both (eventually), but in the main people who write commercial fiction want to get some good income, while literary writers (while welcoming any moolah) want to demonstrate stylistic brilliance (and perhaps win a literary prize).

And though there are exceptions, this remains a general truth: literary fiction doesn't sell as well as commercial fiction.

So what have you got now? The spark of an idea? A *What if?* scenario?

Maybe it's a character who is pinging around in your imagination, dying to get into a story.

Or a story world dying to be central to a plot.

Maybe you've got nothing, absolutely zippo. But you want to write a novel!

Let's see what we can do.

First of all, what is a plot anyway?

It is the record of how a character fights with death through strength of will.

There are three kinds of death. There's physical death, as in most thrillers. But there's also professional death and psychological death.

If the plot is centered upon the character performing the duties of a profession (lawyer, detective), or a calling (mother, father, friend), that character's capacity to continue in that role must be on the line.

The American classic, *Anatomy of a Murder* by Robert Traver, is a courtroom drama. Paul Biegler, the lead, is not being threatened with physical death. He is being threatened with professional death. As a defender of an Army lieutenant accused of murder, Biegler sees himself as an essential part of the machine of justice, of the law itself. As he explains to his client: "[F]or all its lurching and shambling and imbecilities, the law—and only the law—is what keeps our society from bursting apart at the seams, from becoming a snarling jungle ... The law is society's safety valve, its most painless way to achieve social catharsis; any other way lies anarchy."

His client says, "I didn't know you cared."

Biegler, the first-person narrator of the book, reflects, *I hadn't quite known myself how much I cared.*

The law is a holy calling for Biegler, and what happens in the book will challenge his ability to seek justice under the law.

And what about psychological death? We often say someone has "died on the inside." This is often what is found in the best literary fiction, like *The Catcher in the Rye.* But it is also the secret to the category romance. It must seem to the reader that if the two lovers do not get together, their lives will never be whole. Or if they had never met, they would never know true love. Like in *The Bridges of Madison County.*

"They had four days together, just four. Out of a lifetime. It was when we went to that ridiculous state fair in Illinois. Look at the picture of Mom. I never saw her like that. She's so beautiful, and it's not the photograph. It's what he did for her. Just look at her; she's wild and free. Her hair's blowing in the wind, her ace is alive."

Without a life-threatening plot, a character just sits around. I don't care how quirky you make her, she's going to wear out her welcome very soon. The only thing that will save her is the challenge that comes from plot.

Add to the death stakes the main character's strength of will. As Lajos Egri states in his classic, *The Art of Dramatic Writing*:

A weak character cannot carry the burden of protracted conflict in a play. He cannot support a play. We are forced, then, to discard such a character as a protagonist ... the dramatist needs not only characters who are willing to put up a fight for their convictions. He needs characters who have the strength, the stamina, to carry this fight to its logical conclusion.

John Howard Lawson, a famous playwright and screenwriter from the 1930s and 40s, defined drama as "conflict in which the conscious will, exerted for the accomplishment of specific and understandable aims, is sufficiently strong to bring the conflict to a point of crisis."

Your plot has to *feel* like life-and-death to the Lead character who is going to take some sort of action. If you've got that much, you've got, at least, the *makings* of a plot.

TRY THIS:

1. Come up with a potential Lead character for your idea.
2. Write a 500 word biography for this character.
3. Using the character's past and present, define how your plot will involve the character in a struggle against one kind of death: physical, professional, or psychological.
4. Make a list of potential actions the character might take to fight the death stakes.

AREN'T CHARACTERS MORE
IMPORTANT THAN PLOT?

PLOTMAN HAS USED his super hearing to listen in on scores of discussions among writers, writing teachers, agents and editors. Many a time he has heard comments like the following:

All fiction is character-driven.

It's characters that make the book.

Readers care about characters, not plot.

Don't talk to me about plot. I want to follow my characters wherever they lead!

Such comments are usually followed by nods, murmurs of *That's right* and *I so agree.*

To which Plotman says, "Harrumph!" (Plotman believes in a good, old-fashioned *Harrumph.*)

First, we all agree that the best books, the most memorable novels, are a combination of terrific characters and intriguing plot developments.

Second, we all know there are different *approaches* to writing the novel. There are those who begin with a character and just start winging it. Ray Bradbury was perhaps the most famous proponent of this method. He said he liked to let a character go running off as he simply followed the "footprints in the snow." Only later would he look back and try to find the pattern in the prints.

Other writers like to begin with a strong *What if?* plot idea, then people it with memorable characters. Stephen King falls into this category.

So I'm not talking about approaches or methods here. What I am asserting, however, is that no successful novel is ever "just about characters."

In fact, no true character can even exist without plot!

Why not? *Because true character is only revealed in crisis.*

Without crisis, a character can wear a mask. The function of plot is to create crisis so as to rip off the mask and force the character to transform—or resist transforming (as in a tragedy).

What is usually meant by a so-called character-driven novel is that it's more concerned with the inner life and emotions and growth of a character. Whereas a plot-driven novel is more about action and twists and turns (though the best of these weave in great character work, too).

There is some sort of indefinable demarcation point where one can start to talk about a novel being one or the other. Somewhere between James Patterson and Annie Proulx is that line. Look for it if you dare.

We can also talk about the challenge to a character being rather "quiet." Take a Jan Karon book. Father Tim is not facing armed assassins. But he does face the challenge of restoring a nativity scene in time for Christmas. If he didn't have that challenge (with the pressure of time, pastoral duties, and lack of artistic skills) we would simply have a picture of a nice parish priest who we get bored with after about twenty pages. Instead, we have the bestseller *Shepherds Abiding.*

If you still feel that voice within you protesting that it's "all about character," let me offer you this thought experiment. Let's imagine we are reading a novel about an antebellum girl who has mesmerizing green eyes and likes to flirt with the local boys.

Let's call her, oh, Scarlett.

We meet her on the front porch of her large Southern home chatting with the Tarleton twins. "I just can't decide which of you is the more handsome," she says. "And remember, I want to eat barbecue with you!"

Ten pages later we are at an estate called Twelve Oaks. Big barbecue going on. Scarlett goes around flirting with the men. She also asks one of her friends who that man is who's giving her the eye.

"Which one?" her friend says.

"That one," says Scarlett. "The one who looks like Clark Gable."

"Oh, that's Rhett Butler from Charleston. Stay away from him."

"I certainly will," says Scarlett.

The character of Rhett Butler never appears again.

Scarlett then finds Ashley Wilkes and coaxes him into the library.

"I love you," she says.

"I love you too," Ashley says. "Let's get married."

So they do.

One hundred pages later, Scarlett says, "I really do love you, Ashley."

Ashley says, "I love you, Scarlett. Isn't it grand how wonderful our life is?"

At which point a reader who has been very patient tosses the book across the room and says, "Frankly, dear author, I don't give a damn."

What's missing? Challenge. Threat. Crisis. Plot! In the first few pages Scarlett should find out Ashley is engaged to another woman! And then she should confront him, and slap him, and then break a vase over the head of that scalawag who looks like Clark

Gable! Oh yes, and then a little something called the Civil War needs to break out.

These developments rip off Scarlett's genteel mask and begin to show us what she's really made of.

That is what makes a novel.

Yes, yes, you must create a character the readers bond with and care about. But guess what's the best way to do that? No, it's not backstory. Or a quirky way of talking. It's by putting the character into a plot filled with trouble.

So don't tell me that character is *more* important than plot. It's actually the other way around! Thus:

1. If you like to conceive of a character first, don't do it in a vacuum. Imagine that character reacting to crisis. Play within the movie theater of your mind, creating various scenes of great tension, even if you never use them in the novel. Why? Because this exercise will begin to reveal who your character really is.

2. Disturb your character on the opening page. It can be anything that is out of the ordinary, doesn't quite fit, portends trouble. Even in literary fiction. A woman wakes up and her husband isn't in their bed (*Blue Shoe by Anne Lamott*). Readers bond with characters experiencing immediate disquiet, confusion, confrontation, trouble.

3. Act first, explain later. The temptation for the character-leaning writer is to spend too many early pages giving us backstory and exposition. Pare that down so the story can get moving. I like to advise three sentences of backstory in the first ten pages, used all at once or spread around. Then three paragraphs in the next ten pages. Try this as an experiment and see how much better your openings flow.

4. If you're writing along and start to get lost, and wonder what the heck your story is supposed to be about, then brainstorm what may be the most important plot beat of all, the Mirror Moment (please see the chapter "But I'm not a plot planner!" for more on this).

Once you know that, you can ratchet up everything else in the novel to reflect it.

Do these things and guess what? You'll be a plotter!

And that's nothing to be ashamed of. Successful writers in the past bore that label with pride.

I DON'T KNOW IF MY PLOT IS READY

SO WHAT IF you have a plot idea roiling around inside you? And you have tested it to see that there are a) death stakes; and b) a lead character who will demonstrate strength of will?

It's time for EAO.

That stands for: Elevator pitch, Ad line, and One word.

ELEVATOR PITCH

The name for this comes from the idea that you're riding on an elevator with Steven Spielberg, and he asks what you're working on. You've only got a few floors to tell him.

What you don't say is, "Well, Mr. Spielberg, this is a story that is really close to my heart. And I know it would make a great movie, because it has power and emotion and some great characters. Plus, my mother, who is a tough critic, said it's the best idea she's ever heard."

Bing! Tenth floor. Steven Spielberg says, "Good luck with it," and gets off.

What you need is a short pitch that has everything a Spielberg —or any potential buyer of your book—needs to hear to generate interest.

Guess what? There's a formula for that!

It consists of three sentences.

1. (Character name) is a (vocation) who (immediate goal or desire)
2. But when (doorway of no return event), (Character) is (main confrontation)
3. Now (Character) must (death stakes)

Examples:

Will Connelly is a lawyer on the verge of realizing his dream of becoming a partner at a prestigious San Francisco firm.

But when Will celebrates by picking up a Russian woman at a club, he finds himself at the mercy of a ring of small-time Russian mobsters with designs on a top-secret NSA computer chip Will's client has built.

Now, with the Russians mob, the SEC and the Department of Justice all after him, Will has to find a way to save his professional life and his own skin before everything blows up around him. (*The Insider* by Reece Hirsch)

* * *

Dorothy Gale is a Kansas farm girl who dreams of running away with her dog to a land far, far away.

But when a twister hits the farm, Dorothy and her dog and her house are transported to a land of strange creatures and at least one wicked witch who wants to kill her.

Now, with the help of three unlikely friends—a scarecrow, a tin man, and a lion—Dorothy must find a way to destroy the wicked witch so the great wizard will get her back home.

Work on these three lines until they are pristine and clearly show the death-stakes conflict.

By the way, you can use your written elevator pitch to describe your book on the back cover of a paperback and for online bookstores.

If you use this to pitch orally, at a conference or in an actual elevator, don't memorize it. Use your natural speech pattern to give the gist of the idea:

> *Okay. It's the story of a farm girl who dreams of getting out of Kansas. Too much trouble there. She wants to go someplace far, far away, with her little, dog, too. But a big old twister hits and lifts her and the dog and the whole dang house and drops them into a strange, colorful world with all sorts of creatures, and a wicked witch who wants to kill the girl. She has to get to the big wizard, and a scarecrow, tin man and lion help her out. The big wizard tells her to kill the wicked witch, and then he'll send her back home.*

AN AD LINE

An ad line is a short, pithy encapsulation of the "feel" of the story. It's the sort of thing you find on movie posters.

One of the most famous ad lines was for the 1979 movie *Alien*: *In space no one can hear you scream.*

A suspense thriller by James Scott Bell, *Don't Leave Me*, is about two brothers, the younger of them autistic. When the older brother is targeted by bad guys, the younger brother gets drawn in.

The ad line is: *When they came for him it was time to run. When they came for his brother it was time to fight.*

This ad line can be used at the top of your book description on places like Amazon.

But most importantly, it helps you solidify your plot. It puts the vibe in your head. It will guide you as you write.

ONE WORD

What one word encapsulates the heart of your plot?
Is it about Love? Justice? Loss? Reward?
Figure it out.

Then write that one word on a piece of paper and tape it where you can see it when you write.

Note: this word is subject to change. You may discover another word along the way. That's fine.

Just know that having a word gives you focus and direction.

And it lets you know your plot is ready to write!

TRY THIS:

1. Make a list of five possible one-word descriptions of your plot.
2. Pretend you work at an ad agency, and for each word create two ad lines for your boss.
3. Take the best ad line and use it as the basis for plot brainstorming.

HOW DO I PLAN A PLOT IF
I'M NOT A PLOT PLANNER?

EVERY NOVELIST PLANS. It's just that some plans are better than others.

I'm going to write a novel about a woman who goes back to her hometown to heal. I think I'll start with a scene of her driving in a car.

That's a plan. Not a detailed plan, to be sure, but at least it's something.

I understand the resistance to extensive planning. Some authors think they're wired a certain way, that they can't possibly think of planning things out because it makes their imagination muscles cramp up, and puts a cork in their creativity.

Joy is in the discovering, they say. If they knew what was coming they'd get bored writing it.

So the theory goes.

I have a suggestion for this type of writer: The Golden Triangle plan.

The Golden Triangle is from the book *Write Your Novel From the Middle*. It's based on the premise that knowing your novel's "Mirror Moment" is the key to figuring out what your novel is really all about.

For those unfamiliar with the concept, here is a brief overview.

In the very middle of a good book or movie you will often find a moment when the lead character is taking a look at himself, as if in a mirror (sometimes it will be a literal mirror, as in the movie *Sideways*). Such a moment is of two types.

In one type, the character is forced to look at his life and confront his moral failings. You see this in the middle of *Casablanca*, when the drunken Rick insults the woman he once loved. As soon as she leaves he puts his head down on the table in disgust. He's thinking, "Is this what I've become?" The second half of the movie asks the question, Will Rick overcome this flaw and rejoin the human race—and more specifically, the war effort?

The second type of Mirror Moment is when the character looks at herself and her situation and understands the odds against victory are too great, that death—physical, professional, psychological—is imminent.

That's exactly what Katniss Everdeen figures in the middle of *The Hunger Games*. She says to herself at one point, *This is an okay place to die.*

Or the movie *Now, Voyager* starring Bette Davis. Haven't seen it? Get on the stick! These old movies are a wealth of plot and structure knowledge.

Anyway, in this one Bette Davis plays Charlotte Vale, the daughter of the harsh matriarch of a wealthy New England family. The mother has kept her under her thumb all her life, convincing Charlotte that she's not talented nor attractive, and she'd better just be quiet and live out her life without taking any risks.

Charlotte suffers a nervous breakdown and is put under the care of a psychiatrist named Dr. Jaquith (Claude Rains). When she's brought back to health, he prescribes a cruise, which will be her first real step into the outside world. It does the trick. Charlotte begins to come out of her shell. She even falls in love.

When she gets home from the cruise, Charlotte appears transformed. Which triggers her domineering mother, who is determined to use all her influence and psychological pressure to put Charlotte back in her place.

This is where the Mirror Moment happens. Charlotte is facing psychological death at the hands of her mother. She thinks (implied by her actions and the marvelous acting of Davis), *How can I possibly withstand my own mother, who has controlled me my whole life?*

That, in a nutshell, is what the Mirror Moment is about. The nice thing about it is that a writer can find it for their novel at any stage of the process. Plotters, pantsers, 'tweeners. Whenever you are lost in a manuscript, brainstorm possible MMs. One of them will click.

Now, think of the Mirror Moment as occupying the point of an equilateral triangle. The lower left point represents the character's life before the story begins. What is she like? What has made her like that? What moral flaw does she have? How does this flaw affect others?

The lower right of the triangle is the transformation of the character: how she becomes a new and better person (or, in the case of *The Godfather*, a worse person); or how she has become stronger (that is, still fundamentally the same person, but forced to grow stronger through the conflict of the story, as is the case with Marge Gunderson in the movie *Fargo*).

So for those who think they cannot plan, at least try to formulate the three points on The Golden Triangle. That simple but durable structure will guide you in the right direction for your particular story. And even if you feel you want to veer off into more discovery, go ahead and do it. All you do, after awhile, is reformulate the Triangle's points!

There. You're a plot planner. Don't worry—Plotman won't tell on you!

TRY THIS:

Imagine your Lead character in the middle of the story.

1. What is something the Lead needs to know about himself, but is denying?
2. How are the death stakes becoming clear to the Lead?
3. What is the one thing the Lead's most trusted friend needs to tell him, but he doesn't want to hear?

MY PLOT STARTS TOO SLOW

IT WAS a wise writer who once said that a story begins when you strike the match, not when you lay out the wood. And another, John le Carré, who said, *The cat sat on the mat is not the beginning of the story. The cat sat on the dog's mat, is.*

Beautiful descriptions and lyrical flights of literary fancy can work in the hands of a truly talented writer. But not for long. Readers get connected to a story through characters who are either in trouble, or seemingly about to be caught up in trouble.

Readers want to know who the story is about and why they should care. Caring comes from seeing somebody who is disturbed within their ordinary world.

This disturbance does not have to be "big." It doesn't have to be a car chase or gunfight. It can be anything that carries with it a suggestion of change or challenge or imminent trouble.

It can also open *in medias res.* That's Latin for "in the middle of things." (As opposed to writing *in puris naturalibu*s, or "stark naked," about which I have no advice.)

Many times the context in which *in medias res* is used is the all-important opening chapter. But it also applies to other chapters as well.

My formulation of *in medias res* is *act first, explain later.* You don't need a lot of exposition up front. Most authors, knowing their story world and characters' backgrounds, think the reader also has to have a bunch of that info from the get-go in order to be fully engaged. Wrong. Readers will happily wait a long time for those essentials if what's happening in front of them is tense, exciting, compelling, mysterious, active, or otherwise interesting.

Here's an example from one of John D. MacDonald's Travis McGee novels, *A Purple Place For Dying*. The opening paragraph:

> She took the corner too fast, and it was definitely not much of a road. She drifted it through the corner on the gravel, with one hell of a drop at our left, and then there was a big rock slide where the road should have been. She stomped hard and the drift turned into a rough sideways skid, and I hunched low expecting the white Alpine to trip and roll. But we skidded all the way to the rock and stopped with inches to spare and a great big three feet between the rear end and the drop-off. The skid had killed the engine.

That's *in medias res*. We have some unanswered questions: Who is She? Why is she driving so fast on a gravel road when death is just a few feet to the left? What is McGee doing in that car?

"What a stinking nuisance," Mona Yeoman said.

Okay, at least now we have a name.

The cooling car made tinkling sounds. A noisy bird laughed at us. A lizard sped through the broken rock.
"End of the line?"
"Goodness, no. We can walk it from here. It's a half-mile, I guess. I haven't been up here in ever so long."
"How about my gear?"
"It didn't seem to me you had very much. I guess you might as well bring it along, Mr. McGee. Perhaps you might be able to roll enough of this rock over the edge so you can get the jeep by. Or I can send some men to do it."

"If we're going to keep this as quiet as possible, I better give it a try."

Still more questions. What's this about a jeep? Why does she have the ability to send "some men"? Most of all, why do they have to keep things as quiet as possible?

It is not until the bottom of page two that MacDonald begins to fill in some blanks:

> She had met me at noon at an airport fifty miles away, quite a distance from her home base. She said she had a place I could stay, a very hidden place, and we could do all our talking after we got there. Ever since meeting her I had been trying to figure her out.

So have we! Which is the point. MacDonald dangles little bits for us to chew on, just enough to whet our appetite for more. Which is why we keep reading.

STYLISTIC OPENINGS

But what if you *want* to open with description and style? You certainly can try it, but if you do, *don't hold back*. Be bold. Be memorable. Lay it all on the line. Later, under the cool light of the revision process, you can always tone it down, or cut it and go back to action and disturbance. But at least you will have given it your best shot, as Grace Metalious did in her famous novel *Peyton Place (1956)*:

> Indian summer is like a woman. Ripe, hotly passionate, but fickle, she comes and goes as she pleases so that one is never sure whether she will come at all, nor for how long she will stay. In northern New England, Indian summer puts up a scarlet-tipped hand to hold winter back for a little while. She brings with her the time of the last warm spell, an unchartered season which lives until Winter moves in with its backbone of ice and accoutrements

of leafless trees and hard frozen ground. Those grown old, who have had the youth bled from them by the jagged edged winds of winter, know sorrowfully that Indian summer is a sham to be met with hard-eyed cynicism. But the young wait anxiously, scanning the chill autumn skies for a sign of her coming. And sometimes the old, against all the warnings of better judgment, wait with the young and hopeful, their tired, winter eyes turned heavenward to seek the first traces of a false softening.

One year, early in October, Indian summer came to a town called Peyton Place. Like a laughing, lovely woman Indian summer came and spread herself over the countryside and made everything hurtfully beautiful to the eye.

The book was on the *New York Times* bestseller list for 59 weeks.

If you are writing in first person POV, you can achieve a semi-stylistic opening by giving us the voice and attitude of the narrator. Janet Evanovich's character Stephanie Plum gets right to it on the opening page of *Seven Up:*

For the better part of my childhood, my professional aspirations were simple—I wanted to be an intergalactic princess. I didn't care much about ruling hordes of space people. Mostly I wanted to wear the cape and the sexy boots and carry a cool weapon.

As it happens, the princess thing didn't work out for me, so I went to college and when I graduated I went to work as a lingerie buyer for a chain store. Then *that* didn't work out so I blackmailed my bail bondsman cousin into giving me a job as a bounty hunter. Funny how fate steps in. I never did get the cape or the sexy boots, but I *do* finally have a sort of cool weapon. Well okay, it's a little .38 and I keep it in my cookie jar, but it's still a weapon, right?

I still advise beginning with action, which is defined as a character or characters in motion toward a goal, and some disturbing event. Do that, and you can be as stylish as you want.

A series PI character, for example, usually faces a disturbance early, in the form of a new client. In *Free Fall*, an Elvis Cole PI novel by Robert Crais, we open this way:

> Jennifer Sheridan stood in the door to my office as if she were Fay Wray and I was King Kong and a bunch of black guys in sagebrush tutus were going to tie her down so that I could have my way. It's a look I've seen before, on men as well as women. "I'm a detective, Ms. Sheridan. I'm not going to hurt you. You may even find that you like me." I gave her my best Dudley Do-Right smile. The one with the twinkle.
>
> Jennifer Sheridan said, "Is what we say privileged, Mr. Cole?"

When in doubt about your opening pages: act first, explain later. Save most of the backstory and exposition for later. Hook us with a character in motion, preferably with another character in the scene who can provide some points of conflict.

TRY THIS:

1. Make a copy of your opening chapter and strikethrough all exposition and backstory. Cut any necessary descriptions to one line. See if that edited scene doesn't move better.
2. If you feel you need some essential exposition or backstory, limit yourself to three sentences, either all at once or spaced out, within the first ten pages.
3. Test Chapter 2 as your opening chapter. You might be amazed at how much faster things take off.

I THINK MY PLOT NEEDS A PROLOGUE

WHY DO you think you need a prologue? Could it be that your first chapter is too slow? Are you concerned you won't grab the reader right away?

If that is the case, make your first chapter more disturbing. (See the previous chapter).

But what if you really and truly want a prologue? You like the idea of a grabber. Or you're writing an epic and you want to start with a scene that sets up your world, your characters and their stakes.

Yet you've heard all of the cautions about prologues. It is said of editors and agents that they hate prologues. This may be partially true, perhaps because prologues have been mishandled by so many new writers.

A mishandled prologue is one that is a) not necessary; or b) not interesting.

So if you feel the need for a prologue, there are two rules: a) make it necessary; and b) make it grab.

First, let's go over the six basic types of prologues:

- The literary
- The teaser

- The hero in action
- The antagonist in action
- The world builder
- The backstory

LITERARY PROLOGUE

You have to be really good and really brave to try this type of prologue—just as he cautioned in the previous chapter about stylistic openings. Therefore, keep this type of prologue short. A rule of thumb is one page—250 words or so.

Here is the prologue of Michael Connelly's *The Narrows*.

I think maybe I only know one thing in this world. One thing for sure. And that is that the truth does not set you free. Not like I have heard it said and not like I have said it myself the countless times I sat in small rooms and jail cells and urged ragged men to confess their sins to me. I lied to them, tricked them. The truth does not salvage you or make you whole again. It does not allow you to rise above the burden of lies and secrets and wounds to the heart. The truths I have learned hold me down like chains in a dark room, an underworld of ghosts and victims that slither around me like snakes. It is a place where the truth is not something to look at or behold. It is the place where evil waits. Where it blows breath, every breath, into your mouth and nose until you cannot escape from it. That is what I know. The only thing.

I knew this going in on the day I took the case that would lead me into the narrows. I knew that my life's mission would always take me to the places where evil waits, to the places where the truth that I might find would be an ugly and horrible thing. And still I went without pause. And still I went, not being ready for the moment when evil would come from its waiting place. When it would grab at me like an animal and take me down into the black water.

You'll notice the poetic sound of the words: *lies and secrets and wounds to the heart … like chains in a dark room … ghosts and victims that slither around me like snakes.*

Here's a tip: freewrite this kind of prologue. Overwrite it. Write and write, and then let it rest. Come back and edit it down to your 250 words. Even if you decide not to use this as a prologue, some of the writing can be put in your novel at a high emotional point. Nothing is wasted!

You will also notice the last part of the prologue hints at the case to come. That makes it a hybrid, for it is also a teaser. It hints at a very dark tale to come. So let us consider now…

TEASER PROLOGUE

This type may be the most difficult to pull off, because if it is ham-fisted it can seem like a cheap way to get the reader to flip the page. Of course, that is its very purpose. Keep it short and sweet.

Consider this teaser, from Jeff Abbott's *Inside Man.*

The car tumbled off the cliff, hurtling toward the distant blue shimmer of the water.

The first, instinctive reaction is to draw in, brace yourself for the impact. Brace for, never mind *survive*, the impact.

Next was the peculiar itch in my daredevil's brain, figuring gravity's pull at 9.8 meters per second squared, thinking, We have five seconds before we hit.

In the second of those seconds I felt the gun's cool barrel press hard against my temple, realized my passenger was aiming right at my head in case the crash or the water didn't end me.

That is attention to detail. That is commitment.

Three: The water rushed toward us. I moved forward, reaching, the cool steel barrel staying on my head, my fingers along the floorboard groping for my one chance.

The sky, the water, my last breath, everything blue.

Four: The gun fired.

That's it.

Chapter One begins, *Four Weeks Earlier*.

That's how you tease. (Added bonus: This entire prologue was reproduced on the back of the hardcover jacket. You can do that, too!)

BACKSTORY PROLOGUE

The Sleeping Beauty Killer by Mary Higgins Clark and Alafair Burke, opens with a scene prologue, and a gripping one at that. Immediate disturbance and crisis.

> Will the defendant please rise?
>
> Casey's knees wobbled as she rose from her chair. She stood with perfect posture—shoulders back, gaze ahead—but her feet felt unsteady beneath her.
>
> The defendant. For three weeks, everyone in this courtroom had referred to her as "The defendant." Not Casey. Not her given name, Katherine Carter. Certainly not Mrs. Hunter Raleigh III, the name she would have taken by now if everything had been different.

This woman, Casey, is on trial for murder. The trial has concluded and the jury has reached a verdict. Higgins draws out the tension until the foreperson announces that on count one, the charge of murder, the jury finds the defendant ... (I love how Higgins inserts a minor pause here, drawing out the suspense. The forewoman coughs. The gallery groans!) ... not guilty.

Casey puts her head in her hands, full of relief. She thinks about what she'll do and when she goes home she'll be free. She can have a new start. Maybe she'll get a puppy. Maybe go back to school to get her PhD.

But then she remembers there's more to the verdict. There is an alternate charge, manslaughter. And Casey is pronounced guilty. At the end of the prologue we read:

At least one person believes me, Casey thought. At least Angelo believes I'm innocent. But I'm going to prison anyway, for a long time, just as the prosecutor promised. My life is over.

Chapter one begins fifteen years later as Casey walks out of prison.

THE WORLD BUILDER

This type of prologue is usually reserved for epic-sized fiction. It sets a stage. It prepares the expanse.

Brandon Sanderson's *Mistborn* trilogy is huge. Thus he indulges *two* types of prologues: the teaser and the world builder.

Book One, *The Final Empire*, opens with this (italic in original):

Sometimes I worry that I'm not the hero everyone thinks I am.

The philosophers assure me that this is the time, that the signs have been met. But I still wonder if they have the wrong man. So many people depend on me. They say I will hold the future of the entire world on my arms.

What would they think if they knew that their champion—the Hero of Ages, their savior—doubted himself? Perhaps they wouldn't be shocked at all. In a way, this is what worries me most. Maybe, in their hearts, they wonder —just as I do.

When they see me, do they see a liar?

Next comes the prologue proper, which is comprised of three scenes in different, third-person points-of-view. Sanderson skillfully weaves in his world building by placing it within the actions of actual characters.

We learn certain terms—like *skaa* and *koloss*—and find out about the setting—plantation, manor houses. And the class system that includes Lord Rulers and Steel Inquisitors. Also some history, as in:

He had heard whispers of times when once, long ago, the sun had not been red. Times when the sky had been clogged by smoke and ash, when plants hadn't struggled to grow, and when skaa hadn't been slaves. Times before the Lord Ruler. Those days, however, were nearly forgotten. Even the legends were growing vague.

And on it goes, until the final line, *New days indeed*.

The lesson here is combining world building with a real scene or scenes.

But an epic, world-building prologue can also be via straight, omniscient narration.

FLUMMOX THE GATEKEEPERS

As suggested earlier, there are some agents and editors who harbor an antipathy toward prologues. There is a very simple solution to this: *Don't label it "Prologue"!*

Instead, you can:

1. Leave the heading blank. Pure white space. That's what Harlan Coben does in *Tell No One*. After the prologue (that isn't labeled a prologue) he begins with Chapter One, *Eight Years Later*.
2. Use a time or date stamp, e.g., *12:45 a.m.* or *Tuesday* or *Budapest, 1941*.
3. Use 0 instead of 1. That's what Jeff Abbott does with his teaser in *Inside Man*. Clever!
4. Or just call it Chapter 1!

DOES MY PLOT REALLY NEED STRUCTURE?

I'VE HEARD many variations on the following theme:

> *I don't need to think about structure. I don't want to think about structure! I just want to write. I know that if I start writing I'll get to an ending sometime. Stephen King told me that! All structure does is get in the way of my creativity! And I'm just not wired that way. I don't like being told there is such a thing as the three-act structure. How arbitrary! What a stifling of my creativity!*

Indeed, I've even heard writing "teachers" say similar things. And yet when you look at their novels (if, indeed, they have written any) you will find they have a beginning, a middle, and an end.

Imagine that.

Why would this be?

Because unless you want to write an experimental novel you must recognize that readers relate to the story world through structure. Even if you mess around with the order (as in the movie *Memento*), the reader will still be attempting to fit everything into a three-act pattern.

Here's the truth: Story is in the heart concealed, plot and structure are story revealed.

There really is no such thing as story without structure. Think about it. Whenever you write a sentence, you're using structure. If you don't, you're writing nonsense. Or experimental fiction. And you know what the definition of experimental fiction is, don't you? Fiction that doesn't sell. If that's your aim, you don't need plot.

If plot is the record of how a character battles against some form of death, then structure is how you render the plot in a way that readers can best relate to it.

What did you say? Formula?

Let me ask you a question. If someone comes into a restaurant and orders an omelet, do they want a bowl of cucumbers? Or do they want something made by a certain formula? Meaning eggs, heat, and ingredients.

They want an omelet. You make an omelet by a formula. What makes an omelet unique to each chef are the spices and cheeses and veggies and meats they choose to put in, and in what amounts.

That's the secret of writing gripping fiction, too!

Beginning, middle, and end. With spices and cheeses and veggies and meats in each section.

But Shakespeare wrote in five acts!

Nay, knave, not so! What he called "acts" were divisions according to the fashion of the time, but when you look upon the whole play, it fits perfectly into three acts.

I divide the three acts by way of two "doorways of no return." That is, no later than 25% in (for novels, I actually recommend 20%) the protagonist is forced (by circumstance or emotion or some combination of the two) into the conflict of Act 2. He must go through a doorway that does not allow a return back to the "ordinary world." He must continue forward in the "death struggle" which he will either win or lose. The second act is fully half the book. Then another doorway appears—some clue or discovery, or setback or crisis—which makes inevitable the final battle and resolution of Act 3.

Let's take Romeo, for example. What happens at about the 20% mark of the play?

He falls head over heels in love!

O, she doth teach the torches to burn bright!
>It seems she hangs upon the cheek of night
>Like a rich jewel in an Ethiope's ear;
>Beauty too rich for use, for earth too dear!

There's no going back now. That's once in a lifetime love. It is a doorway of no return. This is going to be about *psychological life or death*, which great love stories always are. Romeo and Juliet must have each other, or they will forever be dead to true love!

Oh yeah, and to add to the conflict, their two families hate each other. No way on earth will they allow these two to get together!

That's the true Act 1.

Now we have the conflict, the struggle, of these two lovers to overcome the hate. They get married in secret. But then the hay hits the fan when Romeo kills Tybalt, Juliet's cousin, because he killed Romeo's best friend, Mercutio. Romeo is sentenced to exile.

The major crisis (the second doorway) happens at the 3/4 mark. Juliet's dad (unaware of the secret marriage of Romeo and Juliet) has arranged for her to marry Paris. And when she tries to get out of it, he says:

Hang thee, young baggage! disobedient wretch!
>I tell thee what: get thee to church o' Thursday,
>Or never after look me in the face.

Act 3 revolves around a plan hatched by Friar Laurence to make everybody think Juliet is dead. Oops. Romeo ends up dead and Juliet ends up dead.

The End ... and it followed The Beginning and The Middle!

Structure looks like a suspension bridge, and is just as solid.

Act 1   Act 2   Act 3

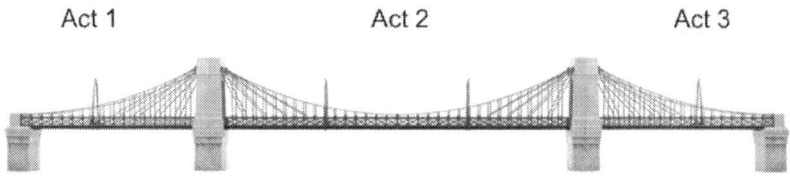

Ah, but now comes the question of *when?* When should I think about structure? What if I am not "wired" to think this way when I start writing? What if I'm a "discoverer"? What if I'm afraid I'll get hemmed in if I try to structure my novel before it's written?

Turn the page for the answer!

WHEN SHOULD I THINK ABOUT THE STRUCTURE OF MY PLOT?

TO BOTH PLOTTERS AND PANTSERS: You should think about structure *when you feel like it* ... just make sure you feel like it *at some point*!

Now that we've got that out of the way, let us consider some misunderstandings.

First, I don't consider "pantser" to be a derogatory term. It actually comes from the lexicon of early aviation, when pilots had to feel the air under the wings by way of the seat. No instruments, no computers. And no full control over where they were going to end up.

Sometimes there was a crash landing, too.

Which is often how a first draft looks to a pantser ("organic writer" or "intuitive writer"). The heart and soul of the story may be there, but now comes the task of translating that to the reader in the best possible way.

Which is what structure is for.

Many successful writers do consider structural form before setting out to write the novel. Some, like James Patterson, have a complete and detailed outline in place. Others use a "step skeleton" outline, which is a short description of one or two lines for each scene. This is often worked out on index cards and placed on a corkboard (physical or digital).

One famous metaphor about writing came from E. L. Doctorow, who said for him writing the novel is like driving at night with the headlights on. You can only see the road ahead as far as the headlights allow. When you drive to that spot, you can see a little further.

If you are a night driver kind of writer, consider driving to the next *signpost*. Each signpost is a structural beat. I identify fourteen signposts which always take you in the right direction. They are:

1. Opening Disturbance. Any kind of change, challenge, trouble, or difference in the Lead's ordinary world. The first scene.

2. Care Package. Someone the Lead cares about as the story begins, part of the Lead's life in the ordinary world. Show the care happening early in the story.

3, Argument Opposed to Transformation. A moment where the Lead states a belief that will be overturned at the end. This is the "thematic line." For example, Dorothy in *The Wizard of Oz* argues (to Toto) that there must be a place with no trouble. Far, far away. At the end, she's learned, "There's no place like home." Rick in *Casablanca* says in the beginning, "I stick my neck out for nobody." At the end, he sacrifices himself for others. (I'll have more to say on this in the chapter "My plot ends with a thud.")

4. Trouble Brewing. Things may settle for a bit after the disturbance, but then a glimpse of greater trouble coming or hovering "in the air."

5. Doorway of No Return #1. Thrusts the Lead into the confrontations of Act II.

6. Kick in the Shins. In trying to solve the problem, achieve the objective, get moving, the Lead suffers a significant setback.

7. The Mirror Moment. (I explain this in the chapter "But I'm not a plot planner!")

8. Pet the Dog. During the troubles of Act II, the Lead takes time out to help someone (or animal!) weaker than himself, even at the cost of more trouble. For example, Dr. Richard Kimble in The Fugitive saves the little boy in the emergency room, even though he gets found out by a nurse who calls security.

9. Doorway of No Return #2. Major setback, crisis, clue, or discovery. Makes final battle necessary and/or possible.

10. Mounting Forces. The opposition—knowing the battle is really on and that the Lead is committed—mounts larger forces.

11. Lights Out. The darkest part of the plot for the Lead. It looks like all is lost.

12. Q Factor. The emotional push that gives the Lead the courage to fight on or make the right choice, by recalling or seeing something of emotional impact from Act I, or hearing from a trusted character about the need to fight or choose rightly. (I call this the "Q Factor" in honor of that character from the James Bond films, who appears early in Act I to explain all the gadgets Bond gets to use. One of the gadgets usually gets Bond out of trouble near the end.)

13. Final Battle. Outer (will Lead overcome the forces?) and/or Inner (will Lead make the right choice?)

14. Transformation. Usually the last chapter of your book, confirming the character's change to stronger self or new self, and carrying the emotional resonance you want to leave with the audience.

Once again: you can plan these out before you write. Or you can wing your way from signpost to signpost. If your story breaks down at any point, just tinker with it until you have at least a notion of what the next signpost might be.

This will keep you driving forward … and prevent you from driving off a cliff.

I THINK I HIT A PLOT WALL

EARLY IN MY writing career I noticed something happening when I got to around the 30k word mark in a manuscript. It was like I hit a wall. It's not that I didn't have ideas or know the direction of the plot. It was just a strange feeling, like I wasn't sure what to write next. I'd look ahead at the 60k or more words I had to write, and got the heebie-jeebies. What the heck was going on?

Luckily, I found out I wasn't alone. Lawrence Block reported the same thing in his book *Writing the Novel*:

> One thing I've come to recognize is that I tend to run into a wall at a certain point in all of my books .... I find myself losing confidence in the book—or, more precisely, in my ability to make it work. The plot seems to be either too simple and straightforward to hold the reader's interest or too complicated to be neatly resolved. I find myself worrying that there's not enough action, that the lead's situation is not sufficiently desperate, that the book has been struck boring while my attention was directed elsewhere.

No less an author than George R. R. Martin has experienced the wall. As of this writing Martin is in the midst of a long patch of writer's delay involving the next book in his *A Song of Ice and Fire* series. In an interview he said:

> I know there are a lot of people out there who are very angry with me that *Winds of Winter* isn't finished. And I'm mad about that myself. I wished I finished it four years ago. I wished it was finished now. But it's not. And I've had dark nights of the soul where I've pounded my head against the keyboard and said, "God, will I ever finish this? The show is going further and further forward and I'm falling further and further behind. What the hell is happening here?"

This sounds like the wall and is completely understandable in light of the complexity of the books, not to mention the TV series running ahead of him!

Patrick Rothfuss, another popular fantasy writer, has also been in the midst of a very public delay for the third novel in his Kingkiller Chronicle (the second book was published back in 2011). In an interview Rothfuss said something interesting:

> "But I am moving forward. More importantly, I'm finally getting my life sorted out so that I can go back and approach my writing and my craft with the joy that I used to feel back in the day, when I was just an idiot kid playing D&D or working on my unpublishable fantasy novel."

Most writers can relate to that. When we first sat down to write a novel, we felt the joy of creation, the pure fun of making stuff up. We shouted *Huzzah!* when we typed *The End* (or something that sounded like *Huzzah*. Maybe it was just *Whew*.)

But then we got the stunning news that what we had written didn't work. We had to figure out why. We had to learn the craft. We had to work.

Then some of us got contracts and had to finish books with the cold, merciless wind of deadlines blowing across the backs of our necks. That chill was even more ominous if we found ourselves at a wall in our manuscript. So I've developed some strategies to prepare for that dreaded moment.

1. THE 20K WORD STEP BACK

At 20k words the foundation of my novel had better be strong. There's a whole lot of words to write, characters to flesh out, plot twists to justify. So stop around 20k to assess:

A. Is my Lead compelling enough? Will readers care about his plight? Is he likable? Does he have qualities with which readers can empathize?

B. Are the stakes death (physical, professional, or psychological)? What can I do to ramp up the stakes?

C. Has my Lead been truly forced through the Doorway of No Return (when the book plunges into Act 2)?

D. Do I have enough of an orchestrated cast? Do my secondary and minor characters have enough uniqueness about them? Are they sufficiently in conflict with other characters?

2. THE JOY FACTOR

"For the first thing a writer should be is—excited," writes Ray Bradbury in *Zen in the Art of Writing*. "He should be a thing of fevers and enthusiasms. Without such vigor, he might as well be out picking peaches or digging ditches; God knows it'd be better for his health."

Clayton Meeker Hamilton, a professor of writing in the early 20th century, believed that an evident "self-enjoyment in the exercise of the sense of narrative" (or, put another way, "the joy of telling tales") operates on the reader in a magical way. "The joy of telling tales which shines through Treasure Island is perhaps the main reason for the continued popularity of the story. The author is having such a good time in telling his tale that he gives us necessarily a good time in reading it." (*A Manual of the Art of Fiction*)

Finding—and keeping—the joy in your story is thus absolutely essential, not just to break through the wall, but to elevate the entire book. That means:

A. Going deeper into characters. This is a source of originality and interest. Giving even a little bit of backstory to minor characters creates all sorts of possibilities. You're more likely to feel joyful when your novel teems with the possible coming out of characters.

B. Make things even harder for the Lead! Stop being so nice. Keep asking: what could make things worse? Oh, yeah? How about worse than that?

C. Keep a novel journal. Begin your writing day by jotting down any thoughts about your plot at the moment, asking questions about it such as "What if?" Write entries to yourself about how you're feeling at this stage. The few minutes it takes to record these things not only keeps you in the story; you can look back at early entries to recapture what got you jazzed in the first place.

3. THE SKIP AHEAD

If you're still feeling hampered or unsure at the wall, get a long pole, back up fifty yards, then run like mad and vault right over the thing. Land a few scenes ahead. Pick the future scene you're most excited about writing. Then write it!

Now, turn around and look backward. You should be able to plot a way to get from the wall to the scene you just wrote.

4. BEST MOVES

Step away from your manuscript. Go find a quiet spot or your favorite coffeehouse table, and use a pad and pen (I find this an aid to creativity).

Write down the names of every major and minor-recurring character in your novel.

Now, dedicate a page to each of these characters, answering the following question: Considering what this character wants in the story, what is the best possible move he or she can make RIGHT NOW?

Please note that most of your characters will be "off-screen" at any given moment in your manuscript. That's okay. They are not inert. They are in the process of planning, conspiring, sneaking, escaping, suffering ... they are all doing or experiencing something. (When characters are off-screen, I call their activities "the shadow story.")

This exercise will give you lots of plot material, scene ideas, and possible twists.

5. THE GUY WITH A GUN

Raymond Chandler once wryly noted, "When in doubt have a man come through a door with a gun in his hand."

Of course it does not have to be a literal man with a gun. It can be any character introduced in some surprising fashion. We're not talking about a one-off character in a scene, but a recurring character who will add complications to the protagonist's life.

When you place a new character in your story, you immediately inherit all of that character's backstory, agendas, secrets, shadow story and so on. Additional scenes arise organically. As you create the new character, ponder a few questions:

1. What can this character do to make life more difficult for my Lead?

2. Can this character bear a secret that will upset my Lead's applecart?

3. Do they still make applecarts? (You may have to do some research)

4. Is there a hidden relationship this character can have with another in my cast?

5. What is this character's agenda?

6. How far is this character willing to go to gain his objective?

7. How can I give this character an even stronger motive?

MY PLOT IS STARTING
TO DRAG

THERE ARE two primary spots where a plot can start to feel draggy.

The first is when Act 1 goes on too long and the author has not brought the story into the death stakes conflict of Act 2.

The other place is anywhere in the book where there is no conflict.

Let's have a look at each.

THE TOO-LONG ACT 1

Remember, a novel is the record of how a character, through strength of will, fights against a form of death. In mythic terms, this is where the character leaves the ordinary world and enters the dark forest.

Now, most people do not want to traipse out into a dark forest and face death. Something has to happen to force them into the fight. A plot event pushes the character through a doorway of no return. That means once outside, the door back to the ordinary world is slammed shut. The only way back is to fight through and overcome death. Then the character, if he so chooses, can go back.

I've already mentioned Scarlett in *Gone With the Wind*. The outbreak of the Civil War pushes her through a doorway of no return. Her comfortable life as a Southern belle is over. She did not choose that event. It was thrust upon her.

Dorothy in *The Wizard of Oz* gets picked up by a twister and dumped in Munchkin Land. She didn't choose that, but there's no way back to Kansas until she defeats a witch who wants to kill her.

Rick in *Casablanca* is just fine with sticking his neck out for nobody, having casual affairs with women, drinking too much, and avoiding all conflict with the Nazis and French police. Then Ilsa Lund, his one great love, the woman he feels betrayed him, comes into his saloon and stirs up the psychological death match: will Rick stay a man who is withdrawn from the community? Or will he recover his humanity?

The doorway of no return in *Casablanca* slams shut because all the characters are stuck in the city. Things will have to get resolved or one or more of them will end up at the wrong end of a firing squad.

Now, the timing of the first doorway is crucial. In most screenwriting instruction, the "plot point" which gets us into Act 2 is placed somewhere around the 25% mark of the script.

For novels, I strongly advise that it come before the 20% mark. That will virtually assure no plot drag at this point.

So can you put this doorway at the 5% or 10% mark? I find this to be too early. Sufficient bonding with the lead character has not fully developed.

Between the gripping opening and the first doorway of no return, get us fully invested in your lead character.

And as you do, keep in mind the lifeblood of fiction—conflict.

WHERE'S THE CONFLICT?

Conflict must pulse through every scene.

Not all conflict needs to be at a 10, but it should never be a 1. You can *start* at 1, but make sure you do something right away to move up the scale. You will always find a level of tension that is fit and proper for a scene.

Take a tip from *Law & Order*. In every episode, the two detectives question several witnesses while investigating a crime. Many of these take place in a work environment, an office or lumberyard or wherever it may be.

Instead of merely having the two detectives talk to somebody in a static manner, the witness is trying to go about his business. He's walking around the office, pulling out files, dealing with memos. Or maybe he's out trying to get a truck to unload some lumber.

The point is there is immediate conflict because the activity itself is interfering with the detectives. Quite often the witness gets testy, which is always a good thing. Testy is conflict! So the detectives have to threaten to take him downtown or use some form of verbal judo to get the guy to talk.

This is what the novelist Elizabeth George calls a "talking head avoidance device," or THAD.

Whenever you have a scene with a lot of talking, look for ways to insert something that will interfere with the talk.

A type of scene that is especially prone to low tension is the sitting down for coffee (or eating) scene. Especially when two people in the scene are on the same side. They are friends or colleagues and they're just talking about what's going on in the story. See if you can insert something relating to the food or the coffee that causes some tension. Have the server interrupt at an inopportune time. Look for ways that one of the allies can have a reason for not wanting to talk. He or she is worried about giving up information, or is holding back a secret. Anything to make the conversation tougher than it would be if two people were just chatting amiably.

CHECK YOUR SCENE STRUCTURE

Structure is every bit as important for a scene as for a book. Readers need to know:

- Who the viewpoint character is.
- What he or she wants, and why it matters.
- What stands in the way of the scene goal.

Now look at your scenes, and ask:

Have I made clear the character's scene goal, either though action, dialogue, or narrative?

Let's use a legal thriller as an example. The plot is about a lawyer defending a rich client who may be guilty. The lawyer needs this case to pay off debt and keep his practice (professional death is on the line).

In chapter four the lawyer gets a lead on a potential eyewitness, someone who might be able to back up his client's story—or blow it apart.

Chapter five opens with the lawyer knocking on the door of the home of the witness. That is an *action*. If you've ended the previous chapter clearly enough, we know what the scene goal is. That's why the lawyer is here, after all. As the scene progresses, the reader will see that goal pursued.

Dialogue can establish a scene goal:

He knocked on the door. A moment later it cracked open. A woman's voice said, "Yes?"

"Mrs. Wingate? I'm Regis Harley. I'm the lawyer representing C. J. Bulkington."

"I already talked to the police."

"If I may have just a few moments of your time—"

"Why should I?"

"Mrs. Wingate, you're the only eyewitness. A man's life is at stake."

Finally, there's straight narrative to clarify a scene goal.

Regis knocked on the door. He took a couple of deep breaths. He couldn't blow this. The woman was the key witness. He had to find out what she saw. Or what she *thought* she saw. Otherwise, he'd be lost as to how to prepare the defense.

It's good to use all three—action, dialogue, narrative—in some combination to establish the scene objective and remind readers what it is at points during the scene.

Now, make sure you have sufficient obstacles to the scene goal. Obstacles come in all shapes and sizes. They can be:

- Personal: when the character is alone, he can struggle with his own inner conflict.
- Interpersonal: another character has an opposing agenda within the scene.
- Physical: something in the setting is getting in the way, e.g., too much traffic to get across town in a hurry; a bridge is out; it's raining too hard.

Make a list of possible obstacles for a scene before you write it. Having written it, look at it and see where you can either add another obstacle or ramp up the tension of an existing one.

For instance, in our legal thriller example Mrs. Wingate is reluctant to talk. What if, during the scene, she has a screaming fit? Or pulls out a gun? Or throws a vase at our lawyer? Brainstorm, come up with five or six possibilities without editing yourself, and see where it all goes.

Finally, end your scene with a page-turning prompt.

Don't let your scenes fall flat at the end. Usually this happens when a scene is written to its logical conclusion. If you end a scene before that, you raise a question in the reader's mind, which then prompts the turning of the page to find the answer.

A good read-on-prompt can be:

- A mysterious line of dialogue.
- An image that is full of portent (like the fog rolling in, or a distant sound).
- A secret suddenly revealed.
- A major decision or vow.
- Announcement of a shattering event.
- Reversal or surprise—new information that turns the story around.

- A question left hanging in the air.

At the very least, when you revise a scene, see what would happen if you snipped the last few lines, or even a paragraph or two. More often than not you'll find a place to end with a bit more momentum than before.

And remember in medias res, "the middle of things." In scene writing, you can start things off with the action in progress, as opposed to "warming up" with descriptive elements. For variety, this can be done in any chapter opening, with the benefit of quickening the pace. Simply give us the action before you give us the setting.

Suppose we have a scene in a judge's chambers between a young lawyer from Dewey, Cheatham & Howe and an angry judge. Let's use first person, with the lawyer as the POV character.

> The next morning I was in Judge Crotchetti's chambers. It had two leather chairs in front of an immaculate mahogany desk, and a floor-to-ceiling bookshelf covering one wall. Judge Crotchetti was standing behind his swivel chair. On the wall above him, an oil-on-canvas Oliver Wendell Holmes glared at me.
>
> "I won't have that in my courtroom!" Crotchetti said, slapping the back of his chair. "Do you understand me, counsel?"
>
> "Clearly," I said, and smiled.
>
> "Young man, are you trying to show contempt for this court?"
>
> "No, Your Honor. I'm doing my best to conceal it."

To quicken the pace, go *in medias res* by leading with the action (note: dialogue is a form of action):

> "I won't have that in my courtroom!" Judge Crotchetti said, slapping the back of his chair. "Do you understand me, counsel?"
>
> "Clearly," I said, and smiled.
>
> "Young man, are you trying to show contempt for this court?"
>
> "No, Your Honor. I'm doing my best to conceal it."
>
> It was Monday morning and we were in Judge Crotchetti's

chambers. It had two leather chairs in front of an immaculate mahogany desk...

When revising, take special notice of the opening paragraphs of each chapter in your book. Do you tend to open the same way? Go for variety. Open with some form of action. Move description further down the page. Get a little more *medias* into your *res*.

SMASH CUT

Another way to speed up the action is by way of the *smash cut*. This is a screenwriting term for a swift and immediate cut from one scene to another, from one action point to another, without a transition in between. Consider this example:

"You won't get away with it," Carrie said.

"We'll see about that," Bob said, and walked out.

So that was the way it was going to be.

She went to the table and picked up her purse. She waited five minutes then took the elevator to the garage and got in her car.

Traffic was thick for some reason, and it took her twice as long to get to the station as usual. She was in no mood for getting blowback from the watch commander.

"Nice of you to drop in," Smedley said.

"Shove it," Carrie said.

There is a narrative transition, explaining how Carrie gets from one scene to the next. From getting her purse to going to the garage to fighting traffic. That's fine, and is perfectly acceptable. But to make things speed up, we can do away with the transition and instead leave a white space on the page to indicate the change:

"You won't get away with it," Carrie said.

"We'll see about that," Bob said, and walked out.

So that was the way it was going to be.

"Nice of you to drop in," Smedley said.

"Shove it," Carrie said. After an hour in traffic she was in no mood for blowback.

Here, the last line gives us the transition information, but only after we're into the scene. The smash cut is a great cinematic tool novelists can use to establish forward momentum.

TRY THIS:

1. Go over every scene in your book and ask yourself how you can ratchet up the tension 10%. Put in more emotion, stronger arguments, inner conflict, frequent interruptions.
2. Look at all your transitions from scene to scene. How many can be eliminated with a smash cut?

MY PLOT IS GETTING AWAY FROM ME

SO HERE'S a question I get from time to time. What do I do if I'm in the middle of my novel and there are so many things happening, and so many characters doing things, that I'm losing my way?

You would think this question would come mostly from the "pantser," the *If I knew what my story was about before I wrote it I'd be bored school of thought*. But it rises with the plotter, too, who has perhaps been overly ambitious about the plans. As sometimes happens for the plot engineers, a sudden twist or turn or character pops in at the 20k mark, one you didn't see coming. The plotter might be tempted to ignore these items, but they shout like Willie Loman's wife: "Attention must be paid!"

So you write on, gamely, only to discover you've a) gone down that infamous rabbit hole; b) are lost in a dark forest; or c) have fallen off a cliff into the bleached bones of the author's graveyard.

Now what?

One wail of frustration is allowed. I advise against a stiff drink at this point, as that may turn into a crutch.

Instead, let's sit down and get a handle on things.

First of all, where are you, as the ad men used to say, "outline wise"? Do not skip over this part, pantsers, for you better have an outline, too.

Wait, what?

I'm talking about a "rolling outline," one you put together as you roll along. When you finish a scene or chapter, write a quick synopsis of who the viewpoint character is, what he wants and what happens, as in: *Ishmael gets depressed, decides to go to sea, and sets off to find a ship.*

I've found the writing program Scrivener to be ideal for this. Your rolling outline can be viewed in both outline form or as index cards on a corkboard. This "birds-eye" view will go a long way to getting a handle on things.

With this in front of you, clarify some crucial matters.

CLEAN HOUSE ON CHARACTERS

How many viewpoint characters have you got? This means you have more than one character with a storyline of their own. For example, in a traditional romance you usually have two viewpoint characters, the lovers. In a long historical or fantasy novel, you may have three or four.

In this case, precisely define the following: What is each character's death-stakes objective? (Please see the chapter "I'm suspicious of plot.") If it's not death, make it so, or drop this as a plotline. In the alternative, consider taking away this character's viewpoint scenes and converting this line into a subplot. This means the character shows up in scenes told from another character's point of view and (this is crucial) complicates the viewpoint character's objective.

For example, you have a woman as a viewpoint character, and a man as another viewpoint character. The man's plotline is not working out in a death-stakes way. You might remove him as a viewpoint, but have him show up in the woman's plotline as a potential lover or long-lost brother or secret agent or alien from a parallel universe.

Clean house. Keep only the crucial characters.

For further study: *The Stand* by Stephen King, and *Strangers* by

Dean Koontz. You'll see how these authors make the several character lines work on their own terms before bringing the strands together.

CUT SCENES THAT DON'T CONNECT TO PLOT

Now that you are squared away on the objective of the main character or characters, assess each scene you've written so far. Ask:

- Does the goal in the scene relate somehow to the overall, death-stakes objective?
- Does the scene present a complication or obstacle to the immediate goal?

Review your elevator pitch, ad line, and one-word summary (see the chapter "I don't know if my plot is ready.")

Note: Subplots are those lines of narrative that intersect with and complicate the main plot. See the chapter "My plot sags in the middle."

TRY THIS:

1. Keep a "rolling outline" of your book. For every chapter or major scene you complete, write a two or three line synopsis of it. What you want is a quick, reviewable record of what you've actually written. (The writing software Scrivener makes this simple. You can write your synopsis on an "index card." Or you can auto-fill the card with the first several lines of your scene.)
2. When you feel your plot is getting away from you, print out the current version of the rolling outline.
3. Find a quiet place where you can spend an hour or so reading the outline and making notes. Think about what each scene means to the overall plot.

4. Brainstorm three directions the plot might go from this point on.

5. Try going back to the point where you felt the plot got off the rails. Brainstorm three different directions from that point.

I'VE HIT A PLOT SNAG

WHAT IS A PLOT SNAG?

It's like when you're walking along admiring some rose bushes and your coat gets impaled by a thorn. Forward motion halted.

With a thorn, all you have to do is unhook your coat. But when you're writing your book, you may not know what to unhook!

A plot snag is not to be confused with writer's block or a loss of enthusiasm for a project. Those are separate issues we'll deal with later.

What we're talking about here is getting to a point in the writing where you don't know what to write next. It doesn't matter if you're a pantser or a plotter or a 'tweener. The best laid plans o' mice and writers often go awry.

Let's say you're writing a thriller and you've got your Lead character backed into a corner. A literal corner, in an abandoned warehouse, where killers are searching for him.

You don't know how your character is going to get out of it.

Snag.

What you do know is that he's going to somehow get in the back of a truck heading for Phoenix.

So what can you do to get him in that doggone truck?

1. MAKE A LIST

Brainstorm possible ways to get out. Go crazy. List six, seven, eight or more. Find the most original option. If you need to plant something in the plot to justify this option (remember how Q always gave Bond the gadgets early in Act 1?) go back and plant.

2. DO SOME SHADOW STORY

The shadow story is what's going on "off-screen." It's what the other characters are doing when they are not involved in the scene you're writing. What did you think? That they were all in their dressing rooms, sipping Coke, waiting to be called?

Brainstorm some of the possible actions going on, and one of them might unsnag you.

3. SKIP AHEAD

If you're stuck but anxious to get on with the writing, skip ahead and write a future scene. Let your subconscious work on the snag. Keep up your writing momentum. Tomorrow or the next day you can come back to fill in the gap.

It's also possible to write a "down and dirty" first draft and avoid plot snags the first time through. You write that first draft like a house afire. And what is the purpose of blazing through? Four things:

1. To discover what your book is about
2. To know if you have the major parts of the plot working.
3. To save time by avoiding endless rabbit trails (are you listening, pantsers?)
4. To identify places where you can fill in material for which you now know the purpose.

Here are some suggestions for you:

SKIP TRANSITIONS

Instead of filling in the information that gets a character from one scene to another, leave a marker in that spot (like *** or &&&) and move on to the next scene. Concentrate on the action and dialogue.

Some writers put in a text reminder in ALL CAPS. For example:

"You'll never make it in time," Wally said.

"Just watch me," Sam said.

SAM GETS TO THE OTHER SIDE OF MANHATTAN, BUT IT ISN'T EASY.

"I'm here," Sam said, fighting for breath.

"Sorry." The deli manager flipped the sign to *Closed*. "I had to give your sandwich to somebody else."

SKIP DESCRIPTIONS

Don't pause for description. Fill that in upon revision. One benefit of this method is that you'll know the overall tone of your novel and how each scene contributes. You can then tailor your descriptions with more efficiency. For example, you know what's coming in the plot, so maybe you'll want to plant a symbol or a clue in the description.

SKIP DEEP EMOTIONAL BEATS

Emotional beats heat up a plot and get us bonded to a character. It's an important part of the craft, and the deeper the emotion the more attention must be paid to it.

When you get to such a moment in your story, jot down the emotion you expect the character to experience. Or a simple reminder to fill it in later, e.g.,

SAM SHOWS HIS ANGER

Or:

SHOW SAM'S EMOTION HERE

Pro tip: When you go back to revisit these moments, look around for a more original emotion than you first suspect. Sure, maybe anger is what you need, but what if you brainstormed other possibilities? Like *elation* or *remorse?* Perhaps one of these other emotions can conflict with the anger, so that you have that great beat called inner conflict.

Another tip: For brainstorming different emotions and techniques for showing them on the page, consult *The Emotion Thesaurus* by Angela Ackerman and Becca Puglisi.

Once you've finished that first draft, you'll discover your writer's subconscious mind (what Stephen King calls "the boys in the basement") will have been working all along filling in those little gaps. You'll be ready to do your "full and fabulous" second draft!

MY PLOT HAS HOLES

GILDA RADNER, the famous comedienne of *Saturday Night Live* fame, did a character named Roseanne Roseannadanna. She'd do some commentary for the news segment, answering mail from a Mr. Richard Feder of Fort Lee, New Jersey. The commentary would eventually devolve into something to do with personal grooming or hygiene, until the new anchor (Jane Curtin) interrupted because she was feeling ill.

One instance had Roseanne Roseannadanna making an analogy to a piece of skin hanging from your lip.

Which is what a plot hole is like.

It's something the reader notices, hanging there. It's distracting and ultimately … disappointing.

There are several kinds of plot holes, from cracks in the sidewalk to craters in the concrete.

The biggest hole, of course, is when a major event in the novel is not brought to proper resolution. At the other end of the spectrum is a plot item that figured in an early scene—like a crucial piece of evidence, or an item of value to one or more characters. If a reader gets to the end of the book and wonders what happened to that pearl necklace from Chapter 5, you have a small hole. But even small holes detract from the pleasure of a novel, just as a pothole in the street takes away from a smooth drive.

How do we fix things? Try using minor characters. They're great for plugging up holes.

Let's say you get to the end and that pearl necklace is still dangling. Your main character and her policeman boyfriend are about to confront the villain. They're at police headquarters making a plan. Now you invent a minor character, a small time crook who's just been arrested. The arresting officer tells the policeman boyfriend that the crook has asked to speak with him.

The crook says, "Maybe you can help me out, huh? Do me a favor?"

"Why should I?" the cop says.

"Maybe I got something you need."

"What could you possibly have?"

"Does a pearl necklace mean anything to you?"

Cop grabs crook's lapels. "What do you know about it?"

The crook goes on to explain how he got the necklace, and from whom. Plot hole plugged up.

You can even go back and plant this character earlier in the novel. Maybe he's a shadowy figure in a scene, who makes an escape. When he comes back at the end, the cop recognizes him from the first encounter.

One of the great things about being a novelist is that you can create a character at any time for any reason. There are innumerable ways minor characters can be used to plug up plot holes.

TRY THIS:

1. Make a list of every plot thread in your book. One line will do.
2. Check off any that are open at the end.
3. See if one of the existing characters can plug the hole. If not, create a minor character to do so.
4. Plant that character earlier in the book.

But what about a plot that has been so twisty and turny that it needs a lot of explanation at the end? How do we keep from making it just a big, old-fashioned talkfest by one character?

That is the subject of the next chapter.

MY PLOT NEEDS A BIG
EXPLANATION AT THE END

IN THE "OLD DAYS" of mystery writing, it was common for the sleuth to gather all the suspects together and explain all the clues before finally fingering the culprit. It was a convention, accepted by mystery lovers who read the genre primarily for the puzzle aspect.

But what if you're writing a thriller with some major twists that need to be explained at the end? Sure, you can have a new character come in and do it in a talky way (think of the psychiatrist at the end of the movie *Psycho*).

A better method is to "hide" the explanation within a scene of actual conflict. To illustrate the point, let's unpack the last section of Dashiell Hammett's classic, *The Maltese Falcon*. (If you are as yet unfamiliar with this book, or the 1941 faithful movie version starring Humphrey Bogart, skip this chapter until you have read it and/or seen it, for there will be spoilers ... and besides, every fiction writer should know *The Maltese Falcon*, which should replace *The Great Gatsby* on high school reading lists!)

The first 5/6ths of the novel revolve around several characters trying to get their hands on a statuette of a falcon of inestimable value. The central character, Samuel Spade, is a private detective operating in San Francisco. At the start of the book he's hired by a woman calling herself Miss Wonderly. She wants Spade to tail a man named Floyd Thursby who, she says, has her long lost sister in tow.

Spade's partner, Miles Archer, likes the looks of Miss Wonderly, and takes the task.

Mistake.

Spade is awakened that night by the cops. Archer is dead, shot. Spade goes down to the scene. Later, the cops arrive at Spade's apartment and start questioning him. Turns out the man Thursby was also shot, about half an hour after Spade left the scene of Archer's death.

Two murders now.

Spade goes to Miss Wonderly's apartment to tell her what's happened, and quickly discerns she's holding out on him. She admits she lied. Her real name is Brigid O'Shaughnessy. She tells Spade she was afraid of Thursby, and doesn't want to be dragged in by the police. She begs Spade to "protect" her.

In his office, Spade is visited by a mysterious little man named Joel Cairo, who thinks Spade may have a bead on "an ornament that has been—shall we say?—mislaid ... the black figure of a bird."

Which is, of course, the falcon. But why it is so valuable we don't learn right away. What we do learn is there's a man named Casper Gutman willing to pay a large sum for its recovery.

From there the plot takes further turns as Spade tries to figure out what's what. Then a sea captain named Jacobi stumbles into Spade's office, full of bullet holes, and holding a parcel. Jacobi dies on the spot, but the parcel is the black bird.

Spade checks the parcel at a bus terminal and mails the ticket to a post office box he uses for business.

Now he has the bird. Now he's ready to strike a deal for it. But he's also got his partner's murder to solve. Since Spade is a suspect in the killings of Archer and Thursby, he's got to find a "fall guy" to take the raps.

Which brings us to the final section of *The Maltese Falcon*. Here all the principal characters gather in Spade's apartment—Brigid O'Shaughnessy, Joel Cairo, Casper Gutman, Spade, and Gutman's "gunsel," a young man (so young he's called a boy) named Wilmer Cook. Spade has been riding Wilmer throughout the book, and the boy really wants to fill Spade full of lead. But he works for Gutman.

This section is virtually all talk, with a bit of action thrown in to keep things interesting. But the task now is for Hammett to let us know how all the parts fit together. Here's how he does it.

1. COLORFUL, ORCHESTRATED CHARACTERS

This is a tip for all of your fiction, but is essential for an explanation scene. The characters all have distinct personalities and physical descriptions.

Spade is a "blonde Satan," who talks in a clipped, hardboiled manner.

Cairo is a smallish dandy with a too-ornate way of speaking. (After he has been roughed up by Spade, he later says to him, "Our conversations in private have not been such that I am anxious to continue them.")

Brigid is beautiful and deceptive.

Gutman is not just fat, he's "flabbily fat with bulbous pink cheeks and lips and chins and neck, with a great soft egg of a belly that was all his torso, and pendant cones for arms and legs."

Wilmer is small and fair-skinned, not very smart but full of bluster.

2. THE EXPLANATION IS PART OF AN ARGUMENT

Spade knows that they all want the bird. That's why Gutman hasn't killed him. Instead, Gutman is willing to pay Spade five thousand dollars for it. But Spade says before that happens "we've got to have a fall guy."

Who is it going to be? Spade suggests Wilmer, Gutman's young gunsel with the hair-trigger temper. Gutman scoffs at the idea! He argues Wilmer is like a son to him. Later, though, when it becomes a matter of actually getting his hands on the black bird, Gutman will indeed give up Wilmer.

3. USE DIALOGUE INTERRUPTIONS

Long blocks of dialogue are hard on readers. Have other characters interrupt or ask questions.

> "That's the choice we'll give him and he'll gobble it up. He wouldn't want to know about the falcon. He'll be tickled pink to persuade himself that anything the punk tells him about it is a lot of chewing-gum, an attempt to muddle things up. Leave that end to me. I can show him that if he starts fooling around trying to gather up everybody he's going to have a tangled case that no jury will be able to make heads or tails of, while if he sticks to the punk he can get a conviction standing on his head."
>
> Gutman wagged his head sidewise in a slow smiling gesture of benign disapproval. "No, sir," he said, "I'm afraid that won't do, won't do at all. I don't see how even this District Attorney of yours can link Thursby and Jacobi and Wilmer together without having to—"
>
> "You don't know district attorneys," Spade told him.

4. USE ACTION INTERRUPTIONS

As Spade has been arguing to make either Wilmer or Joel Cairo the fall guy, Wilmer can't take it. He pulls out a gun, but Gutman and Cairo hold him back.

> Wooden-faced, dreamy-eyed, Spade got up from the sofa and went over to the group. The boy, unable to cope with the weight against him, had stopped struggling. Cairo, still holding the boy's arm, stood partly in front of him, talking to him soothingly. Spade pushed Cairo aside gently and drove his left fist against the boy's chin. The boy's head snapped back as far as it could while his arms were held, and then came forward. Gutman began a

desperate "Here, what—?" Spade drove his right fist against the boy's chin.

5. END THE SECTION WITH A MEMORABLE LINE, IMAGE, OR BOTH

Finally, Spade tells Brigid she is going to take the fall. She killed his partner, and you're just "supposed to do something about it." But just as important, even though he may love her, he's not going to "play the sap" for her. The section ends with the two of them waiting for the police to arrive, and Brigid using all her wiles to get Spade to change his mind:

> She put her face up to his face. Her mouth was slightly open with lips a little thrust out. She whispered: "If you loved me you'd need nothing more on that side."
>
> Spade set the edges of his teeth together and said through them: "I won't play the sap for you."
>
> She put her mouth to his, slowly, her arms around him, and came into his arms. She was in his arms when the doorbell rang.

In the movie, the police take Brigid out to the elevator. Polhaus, Spade's cop friend, asks what this heavy black statuette is. Spade says, "The stuff that dreams are made of."

Out in the hall, bird in hand, Spade watches the elevator cage close as Brigid is taken down to her fate.

TRY THIS:

1. Write out one, long, uninterrupted explanation of your plot.
2. Cut as many lines of the explanation as you can without losing any of the meaning.
3. Render the explanation in dialogue between two or more characters, formulated as an argument.

THERE IS a certain feeling one gets when reading a novel that truly stands out. Perhaps it may best be described as *heart*. It's more than character empathy. It's even more than character sympathy. It's a vibration that permeates the prose.

Heart is not something you can simply lard on with style. You have to dive deep to find it, Then it becomes a matter of feeling it yourself, and letting that feeling emerge naturally on the page.

10 WAYS TO GET TO THE HEART

For these exercises, come up with at least two answers for each (three would be even better!) For each answer, write 250 words exploring them in more detail.

1. **Ghost from the past.** Brainstorm past incidents that can haunt your Lead's present. Choose one. How does it impact her now? Make her feel about herself?

2. **Open wound.** What traumatic experience has put a hole in her soul? What is unhealed inside her that makes her less than she needs to be?

· · ·

3. **Blind spot.** What is it inside her that she doesn't see? What is she trying to avoid by NOT seeing this?

4. **Personal stakes.** What in the story can up the personal stakes for her? Someone close to her in jeopardy? A direct attack on her from the past (see 1-3, above)?

5. **Fatal flaw.** What characteristic does she have that keeps her from victory? What does she do to sabotage herself?

6. **Inner demon.** What is it she fears most? How does this fear freeze her?

7. **Stunted desire.** Is there some deep desire, something she longs for, that has been foreclosed to her? Does she think she's not good enough? Has someone else convinced her of that?

8. **Passion for a cause**. What is it? How does it manifest itself, both positively and negatively, in her?

9. **Stunning loss**. What can she lose that threatens to debilitate her?

10. **Ultimate meaning**. Who or what would your Lead die for?

Put these notes aside for a day, then come back and expand upon them. Set aside for one more day, then edit your notes. Locate the material that most connects with you on an emotional level. Work those material into your book.

5 DEEPENING EXERCISES

For the following exercises, write wild. Don't censor yourself. Let the material emerge and lead where it will. Give at least five minutes to each.

Later, come back to these notes and integrate the most interesting and surprising material into your manuscript. If an exercise leads you to something that might turn your manuscript on its head —good! If it stuns you, it will stun your reader, too.

1. The Third Degree. Put your character in a chair, lights low, except on the chair, like in an old cop show. Now grill him, starting with this question: "What are you trying to hide?" Keep grilling until he breaks.

2. Shocking Coffee. You sit down for coffee with your Lead, and she tells you, "I don't think you've captured me." When you ask why not, she tells you something that shocks you. After you spit out your coffee, she apologizes ... then tells you something even *more* shocking.

3. Closet Search. Imagine someone in your family, or a friend or co-worker, searching through your closet? What is in there that you don't want found? Make it really personal and important. Then transfer that to your Lead.

4. How You Feeling? Go to the end of key scenes. Ask your Lead, "How you feeling?" And let him pour out what's inside him. Write down three actions that *show* that feeling, then three actions that show the opposite. Why the opposite? It's a coping mechanism. Now choose the most original action and work it into the present scene, or the start of the next.

· · ·

5. Chair Throwing. Imagine your character in a nice room with a big, bay window. She picks up a chair and throws it through the window! What would make her do that? Write out a reason. Then write out another reason. What tells you most about this character?

Write a page-long sentence, without stopping, in the character's voice, exploring her emotions.

Now we're getting to it: the beating heart of your novel. Readers will feel the pulse.

MY PLOT ISN'T INTERESTING ENOUGH

YOU'LL OFTEN HEAR readers say a book was *okay.* That means they liked it fine, but it didn't blow them away, and if given a choice between that author and someone new, they are likely to choose the latter.

Your characters and plot may be working on a structural level, yet still remain flat.

So what can you do to avoid this fate? How can you change a plot that isn't all that interesting to one that demands to be read?

By first asking: Where does interest come from?

Answer: Mystery!

And where does dullness come from?

Familiarity!

Want an interesting plot? Then throughout your novel seek to create more mystery and ditch familiarity.

Mystery comes from a reader *not knowing fully* what's going on. Having the answers just out of reach is what makes for a page-turner.

So: Be unpredictable!

There are six primary ways you can ramp up your unpredictability:

1. Twists and Surprises

2. Unpredictable Emotions
3. Settings
4. Professions and Vocations
5. Minor Characters
6. Dialogue

TWISTS AND SURPRISES

A plot *twist* is anything surprising that completely upends the story so far. Like the person you thought was dead turns up alive. Or a close friend is revealed as a traitor. A twist requires the lead character to make major tactical adjustments.

A surprise is simply something the reader didn't see coming because it is so different from what they might expect. For example: A lawyer goes to visit a nice old woman who was a witness to a murder, and after a short conversation she goes into the kitchen to make tea. She returns with a shotgun pointed at the lawyer.

To get twists and surprises, pause every so often in your writing and ask: what would the average reader expect to happen next? Write down the answer.

Come up with other possibilities. Start by thinking of the *very opposite* thing that could happen. Make a list of other possibilities. Now choose the best one and justify it—that is, work into the story whatever you need to make that twist or surprise *understandable in retrospect.*

UNPREDICTABLE EMOTIONS

We all have our typical emotional responses. Someone cuts us off in traffic, we get angry. Someone close to us dies, we grieve. Somebody goes out of his way to hold the door open for us, we are grateful.

Characters coming out of your imagination also have typical responses. They are likely to be very close to what yours would be in a similar circumstance. And readers will not be surprised.

So create an unanticipated emotion. This can then be used either instead of the predictable, or as a means of inner conflict.

Try the opposite exercise. Here's how it goes.

Think of love. How would someone describe their love for another? How does it manifest itself?

Probably in some form of *desire*.

Okay, that's predictable.

What is the opposite of love? Hate, of course. How would that manifest itself? Some form of *aversion*.

What if you worked *both* of those emotions into the heart of a character?

That's what Steve Fisher does in his noir classic, *I Wake Up Screaming* (first published in 1941, and revised in 1960. The latter version is quoted here). The first-person narrator of the book is a Hollywood screenwriter who falls for a beautiful young starlet, Vicky Lynn, who is about to get the studio treatment. She ends up dead, and he becomes a suspect in the murder. The victim's sister, Jill, is there to support him, and as time goes on he starts falling for her. But he doesn't want to!

> But I began thinking of Jill. I tried to fight it but I couldn't. I didn't want to see her. I didn't want to hear her name. But in the middle of a party I would think of her. I would think of the night she sat and listened while I told her how we were going to build up Vicky. I would think of her in my hotel room, wearing that damp linen dress that was tight on her hips. I would think of her in grease paint in a Civil War costume. When I drove in my car and saw the palms and the stars I remembered her. When I kissed girls that didn't mean anything to me at all I remembered Jill. I don't know why. Because I hated her. I was scared, thinking of her.

These cross-currents of emotion are so much more interesting than just a one-note rendition. It really takes us aback. Why hate? Why scared? We read on to find out!

Try the opposite exercise in an early scene. This will pique the reader's interest.

Then try it again in the scene with the greatest emotional pitch.

These two moves alone will elevate the interest level of your novel.

SETTINGS

When it comes to putting our characters into a setting, we often default to the familiar. In a crime novel, for example, there might be a scene set in a bar. Or an abandoned warehouse. We've seen those hundreds of times.

Before you decide on a scene setting, give yourself a minute or two to brainstorm an alternative. Do the opposite exercise here, too. Instead of a dark warehouse, what if the lead and the villain met at a busy hot dog stand in the middle of Manhattan?

One of the most memorable scenes in movie history is the meeting between Holly Martins (Joseph Cotten) and Harry Lime (Orson Welles) in *The Third Man*. Most of the film takes place in shadows and on dark streets. But when Martins meets his old friend Lime, now a notorious racketeer in post-war Vienna, the setting is during the day at an amusement park Ferris wheel. Going up into the air in one of the cars is not only unique among such scenes, but affords all kinds of interesting moves. Such as when Martins wraps his arm around the window after Lime opens the door at the top of the ride. Might Lime really try to throw him out?

That scene is almost always the first one mentioned in discussions of *The Third Man*. One such unique setting in your novel might produce the same effect.

Bonus tip: a setting can also be made more memorable by incorporating the sense of smell. In Jordan Dane's *No One Heard Her Scream*, San Antonio detective Rebecca Montgomery is ordered into her lieutenant's office:

> Lieutenant Santiago's office smelled of coffee and stale smoke, a
> by-product of the old homicide division, before anti-smoking

legislation. Central Station had been smoke-free for quite a while, but the stench lingered from years past, infused into the walls. No amount of renovation had ever managed to eliminate the odor.

PROFESSIONS AND VOCATIONS

Readers love to learn about the ins and outs of unique occupations. Whatever it is your Lead does for a living, render it with specific details. That's one (among many) of the strengths of Michael Connelly's Harry Bosch series. Connelly, a former crime beat reporter in L.A., renders police work with precision and inside information.

But don't forget secondary characters' work. You can go to a database like Occupational Outlook Handbook kept by the Bureau of Labor and Statistics (https://www.bls.gov/ooh) and find a plethora of offbeat things people might do for a living. Then a little research will get you some key details. This always elevates the interest level for readers, so long as you don't do a big dump of information in big block paragraphs. Weave the details in naturally within the action scenes.

MINOR CHARACTERS

Minor characters are a tremendous opportunity to add spice to a novel. Don't waste them by rendering stereotypes. Always look for a fresh angle, an offbeat take.

The primary ways to do that are through description and dialogue.

Give each minor character one memorable trait that can be expressed visually. Here is how Moose Malloy is introduced in Raymond Chandler's *Farewell, My Lovely*:

> *He was a big man but not more than six feet five inches tall and not wider than a beer truck.*

A little later, Philip Marlowe, the narrator, describes Malloy as having *a hand I could have sat in.*

In addition to a visual tag, give each minor character a unique way of speaking, enough to distinguish him or her from the rest of the cast.

There's even a character that's a *minor* minor—the kind that appears only for a moment because he or she is necessary for a scene. Like a doorman or a receptionist. Even they can have a small physical or verbal quirk that sets them apart from the banal.

The doorman can push his chest out like a general.

The receptionist can have eyes like frozen daiquiris.

And the reader can have a moment of fictional delight.

DIALOGUE

The fastest way to improve a manuscript is dialogue.

Crisp, tense dialogue is always interesting to a reader. It gives them a subconscious trust in the writer. It gives emotional kick to the story. Two quick tips:

1. Break up longish dialogue with interruptions

Instead of:

> "I was thinking of going to the police. Not that I have any real evidence, you understand. Just that I feel it is my duty as a citizen to report wrongdoing. And that's what I intend to do."

Try this:

> "I was thinking of going to the police. Not that I have any real evidence, you understand. Just that I feel it is my duty—"
>
> "Nuts to that."
>
> "My duty as a citizen to report wrongdoing. And that's what I intend to do."

Note that an interruption is always with an em-dash, a close quote mark, and the immediate dialogue of the other character. The ellipsis (...) is for when a voice trails off.

"I was thinking of going to the police. Not that I have any real evidence, you understand. Just that I feel it is my ..."
"Your what?"
"My duty as a citizen."

2. Cut flab words. You find a lot of these at the beginning of dialogue

Instead of:

"Are you comfortable?"
"No. These chairs aren't exactly plush."

Try this:

"Comfortable?"
"These chairs aren't exactly plush."

THE AMOUNT of enjoyment a reader gets from a novel is directly proportional to the number of times she is pleasantly surprised by the plot.

Conversely, if a reader guesses what is going to happen, or what a character is going to say, and it does so occur, a moment of reading pleasure is lost to a bit of disappointment. Readers do not like to anticipate and then experience what they anticipated.

They love being fooled, on both large and small scales.

One habit you can develop is that of *unanticipation*.

Every so often stop and ask yourself what the average reader would expect to happen next. You can do this because you are also a reader and, having read millions of words and watched countless hours of movies and television shows, you know what all the standard and clichéd developments are.

Make a list of them.

Now make a list of several options that are the opposite of the expected, or at least put a new spin on them.

Do this when you outline (if you outline) your plot.

Do this before you write a scene.

Do this when you end a scene and think about the next scene.

Do this *within* a scene using something I call SUES—Something Unexpected in Every Scene.

It can be anything from a bit of dialogue to a new character barging in with a gun to an earthquake. Surprises make for happy readers.

These surprises can be brainstormed before you write a scene or pop into your head while you're writing.

A word on dialogue. Don't always be "on the nose." That means the characters using direct responses. You'll do a lot of that, because that's how we communicate in life, and your characters wouldn't be able to function very well without them.

But for variety, and the unexpected, mix in some "off the nose" dialogue.

Example:

"Are you ready to go?" Susan said.

"All ready," Jack said. "What's our first stop?"

"Well, first we'll check the movie theater, then the market. After that the hotel."

"Sounds good," Jack said.

"Anything else you can think of?" Susan asked.

"Not at the moment," Jack said. "Shall we?"

"Absolutely," Susan said.

This dialogue gets across some information, but it is a ping-pong exchange of direct responses. How can you spice this up?

Try answering a question with a question:

"Are you ready to go?" Susan said.

"Is that what you're wearing?" Jack said.

Or sidestep the response altogether:

"Anything else you can think of?" Susan asked.

"Ghandi was nuts," Jack said.

Why did Jack say that? Figure it out and work it into the scene!

I'll even take a novel off the shelf, open to a random page, and select a random line of dialogue. I'll then ask, what if this line were in the scene I'm writing? Or a line similar to it, which I tweak a little bit?

This usually suggests a whole new direction to the scene, or perhaps indicates a bit of backstory that can be woven in.

All this brainstorming will help train your mind for SUES.

TRY THIS:

1. Take a favorite novel and read a few chapter endings.
2. Ask: how could the author have ended each chapter with more of a shock or surprise? Create at least two alternatives for each.
3. Now run the same exercise for your own chapters.

MY PLOT ISN'T GRIPPING ENOUGH

WHAT IF YOU get the feeling that your plot is sound and your characters compelling, but something about it feels, well, flat?

Or you give it to a beta reader for feedback, and get the response, "Hey, it was pretty good."

And you say, "Only pretty good? What's missing?"

"I can't quite put my finger on it."

Talk about frustrating!

Here's what to do.

USE ACTIVE VOICE

Examine your prose to see if you're using *active voice* in your sentences.

If you didn't like grammar in school, then at least learn to identify and utilize active voice. It will go a long way toward making your prose more accessible and exciting—more gripping—to readers.

So what is active voice? Okay, here you have to get a little grammatical. Don't let it freak you out. It's really pretty simple.

In the active voice, the SUBJECT of the sentence DOES something. The SUBJECT is the noun and the DOES is the verb.

If you keep the subject-noun in front of the verb, you're in active voice. If you put the noun after the verb, you're in a passive voice.

Active example:

John pounded the table.

The SUBJECT (John) pounded (VERB) the table. That's active voice.

But this is passive:

The table was pounded by John.

See how the VERB is now in front of John?

(Not to get too technical, but the passive sentence makes the table the actual subject of the sentence, but this will mess with your mind.)

As a general guideline, then, just ask yourself who is the most important person in the sentence, or what is the most important thing, and put that person or thing at the front of the sentence, with the verb after it.

The door was plowed into by the car (passive).

The car plowed into the door (active).

The gun was held by Steve (passive).

Steve held the gun (active).

Related to active voice is the use of strong, vivid verbs. In the last example, a better sentence would be: *Steve gripped the gun.* Or get creative with something like: *Steve white-knuckled the gun.*

If you find yourself propping up a verb with an adverb, it usually means you need a stronger verb.

Jane hit Sam roughly. (*hit* is generic)

Jane slapped Sam. (Better. Vivid, and no adverb necessary)

SHOWING VS. TELLING

There is abundant instruction out there on showing vs. telling. An hour spent on the internet will get you most of what you need to understand the subject. It's essential not only to know the difference, but when to use one or the other.

For if you *tell* when you should *show*, the story slows down and fails to grab. But you also can't *show* everything or you'll do five pages on someone crossing a room to open a window.

I developed a simple tool called the Intensity Scale. Basically, you imagine a scene in terms of intensity, or heat. The lowest heat (meaning lack of conflict) is a 1. The highest intensity is 10. Your scenes should be between 2 and 9, usually on an ascending scale. When your scene is at a 5 or above, specialize in showing. When you're below a 5, you can do more telling.

You want to use telling to get you, as quickly as possible, into the show zone.

For example:

Mary walked into the room and sat down.

"I'm glad you came," Frank said.

"Sure," Mary said, trying to keep her impatience from getting the best of her.

That's telling us what Mary is feeling. It's fine, because we're under 5 in the intensity scale. The heart of the scene is yet to come. It builds, until Mary is furious.

She stood and slapped Frank across the face.

That's showing. It's not, *Mary was furious.* Instead, we *see* what Mary is through her actions.

If your plot isn't gripping, check your show and tell.

SENSORY DETAILS

Since we're a visual-aural culture, writers naturally tend to stress the senses of *sight* and *sound* in their fiction. Which is as it should be. It's the primary way readers visualize what's going on in a scene.

But some judicious dollops of the other senses—*taste, touch,* and *smell*—will draw a reader further in.

Before you write a scene, do a quick brainstorm for all five senses. Come up with two or three possibilities for each. Choose the best ones and weave them in.

Often overlooked is the sense of smell. Who can forget Robert Duvall's speech in *Apocalypse Now*? Playing a commanding officer who leads the fiery destruction of a Vietnamese village, Duvall takes a deep breath and tells a soldier:

> I love the smell of napalm in the morning. One time we had a hill bombed for twelve hours. When it was all over, I walked up. We didn't find one stinking dink body. But the smell! You know, that gasoline smell. The whole hill. It smelled like ... victory.

As an exercise, look at several of your scenes and highlight the sensory details. Use different colors for sight, sound, taste, touch, and smell. If the scenes are dominated by only one or two senses, work in some others. This will add to that mysterious "grip" factor that's been missing.

BE WISE WITH ADJECTIVES AND ADVERBS

The famous editor Sol Stein called nonessential adjectives and adverbs "flab," and prescribed liposuctioning them out:

> The quickest way of increasing the pace of a manuscript and strengthening it at the same time is to remove all adjectives and adverbs and then readmit the necessary few after careful testing. (*Stein on Writing*).

Adjectives and adverbs are *modifiers*. Adjectives help out a noun, and adverbs help out a verb.

For example, a *car* is a noun. Adding an adjective of color (*a red car*) or motion (*a fast car*) gives us more specific information about that noun. (The two adjectives Stein says you should always drop are *very* and *quite*. These of course may be used in *dialogue* if consistent with how a character talks.)

To walk or look or chew are verbs (describing action). Adverbs are added to give us more information about how the action is done:

He walked away *angrily*. (The adverb can also be placed before the verb: He *angrily* walked away.)

He looked at me *warily*.

He chewed *loudly*.

What you should train yourself to do is look at your adverbs and see if you can choose a more vivid verb. As in:

He *stormed* away.

He *studied* me.

He *chomped*.

Be especially wary of adverbs in dialogue attributions:

"I hate you!" John said angrily.

"I will not eat that!" Sally said petulantly.

"Oh, all right, you can have it," Stan said begrudgingly.

Instead, *shape* the dialogue so the tone is obvious, and/or add action to the scene to make it clear:

John balled his hands into fists. "I hate you."

Sally shook her head. "I will not eat that!"

Stan sighed and held out the Tupperware. "Oh, all right, you can have it."

All the suggestions in this chapter are to help you move your plot from good to gripping. No more "I liked it fine" remarks from readers. Go for "I couldn't put it down!"

MY PLOT ISN'T STYLISH
ENOUGH

NOT EVERY WRITER is interested in *style*. If they can write lean, mean plots that move, with interesting characters and a satisfying ending, that's enough. They'd rather write fast and turn out more work than spend extra time trying to find the "right" words.

Isaac Asimov was such a writer. He purposely developed a stripped-down style so he could churn out the books. He was once asked what he would do if he found out he had just six months to live. "Type faster," he said.

Other writers do seek to enhance their prose. One such was John D. MacDonald, considered one of the great crime writers of the 20th century. He wrote a string of paperback classics in the 1950s, and then invented an enduring series character for the 60s and beyond—Travis McGee.

He was a great plotter, but a careful stylist as well. As he himself once put it: "I want a bit of magic in the prose style, a bit of unobtrusive poetry. I want to have words and phrases really sing."

Here's an example from one of his McGee novels, *Darker Than Amber*:

She sat up slowly, looked in turn at each of us, and her dark eyes were like twin entrances to two deep caves. Nothing lived in those caves. Maybe something had, once upon a time. There were piles of picked bones back in there, some scribbling on the walls, and some gray ash where the fires had been.

While "unobtrusive poetry" is not necessary for a well-plotted novel, it is an *elevation*. It's a fine thing to consider stretching your prose. The main proviso is that you never let the style overplay its hand. Serve the story first.

One place where prose style is most fitting is when there is a high emotional moment. Nothing is higher than a young writer dying, in the aptly titled and justifiably famous short story that made William Saroyan's reputation, "The Daring Young Man on the Flying Trapeze."

> Then swiftly, neatly, with the grace of the young man on the trapeze, he was gone from his body. For an eternal moment he was all things at once: the bird, the fish, the rodent, the reptile, and man. An ocean of print undulated endlessly and darkly before him. The city burned. The herded crowd rioted. The earth circled away, and knowing that he did so, he turned his lost face to the empty sky and became dreamless, unalive, perfect.

Stretch your prose in the safety of your own writing room, and that muscle will be there for you when you write.

Three ideas for you:

1. READ POETRY

Ray Bradbury, one of our greatest unobtrusive poet-writers, read some poetry every day. "Poetry is good because it flexes muscles you don't use often enough," Bradbury says in *Zen in the Art of Writing.* "Poetry expands the senses and keeps them in prime condition."

2. WRITE PAGE-LONG SENTENCES

As an exercise from time to time, write a run-on sentence of 250 words or so. Don't edit yourself. Let the words take you wherever they roam!

This is a good way to add emotional depth to a scene. When you get to a point where you describe emotion, start a fresh document and write a page-long sentence of inner description. Don't judge it; just write it.

When you're done, look it over. Maybe you'll use most of it in your novel. Maybe only one line. But what you'll have is fresh and stylistically pleasing. I'm certain this is how Jack Kerouac came up with that famous passage in his novel *On the Road:*

> The only people for me are the mad ones, the ones who are mad to live, mad to talk, mad to be saved, desirous of everything at the same time, the ones who never yawn or say a commonplace thing, but burn, burn, burn like fabulous yellow roman candles exploding like spiders across the stars and in the middle you see the blue centerlight pop and everybody goes "Awww!"

3. PLAY WITH METAPHORS

Dow Mossman, author of *The Stones of Summer* (the subject of a documentary, *The Stone Reader)* says he considered each page of his massive novel to be its own poem. Naturally it is filled with metaphors and similes.

> He stood, leaning against the wooden jamb of the double glass doorway, looking back, and his eyes seemed almost dull, flatter than last year, muted somehow like reptiles not swimming in open water anymore.

Dull eyes like *reptiles not swimming* surprises in a pleasing way, but also fits the overall tone of the novel. The best similes and metaphors do both.

So how do you find these images?

Make a list. At the top, write the subject. In the above example, it would be *dull eyes*. Dull like what?

List as many images as you can, absurd and farfetched as they may be. Push past your comfort zone. Force yourself to come up with twenty possibilities. One of them will surely work.

Robert Newton Peck uses nouns in place of adjectives to plant the unexpected in his novel *A Day No Pigs Would Die:*

> *She was getting bigger than August.*

> *The whole sky was pink and peaches.*

Like Peck, you should occasionally step outside the normal, grammatical box. You'll find some pleasant surprises when you do.

You can also take familiar expressions and glitz them up. This is called *curving the language*. Write out a description as it comes to you, as banal or cliché-ridden as that may be, and then find ways to make it fresh.

For example, you write, "She was beautiful." Now you start to play with it, adding or changing words along the way. You might jump immediately to the cliché, "She looked like a million dollars."

Harlan Ellison came to this point, and ended up with, "She looked like a million bucks tax free." That little addition at the end makes this a fresh expression.

DO THE CHANDLER

Raymond Chandler was the greatest genre stylist of all time. His Philip Marlowe novels—such as *The Big Sleep, Farewell, My Lovely, The High Window* and *The Long Goodbye*—are still revered for their seemingly effortless and unobtrusive poetry. Lines like:

> It was a blonde. A blonde to make a bishop kick a hole in a stained-glass window.

She gave me a smile I could feel in my hip pocket.

I lit a cigarette. It tasted like a plumber's handkerchief.

These melodious lines did not roll off, fully formed, from the fingertips of the master. He typed on half sheets of paper in order to force himself to write memorably on each sheet before moving on.

It's a "trick" that you can use by upping your page view to 200% or so and working on just that much of your page.

MY PLOT IS IMPLAUSIBLE

ON OCCASION A WRITER may worry that a reader will find something in the plot implausible.

It's a valid concern, because implausibility—the sound of the reader muttering (or screaming) "Oh, come on!"—ruins the fictive dream.

I recall an opening chapter in a thriller in which a federal SWAT team swoops down on a suburban home in the dead of night, breaks in, nabs the sleepy occupant and takes him into custody. (What all the hubbub and flashing lights and helicopters do to all the neighbors is never explored.) So why did the feds go to all this trouble to nail this guy with all their tactical resources and skills? Because there's a notorious criminal in fed custody who says he'll only talk to this guy. That's why the feds have brought him in.

At which point one is justified in asking why an FBI agent did not wait until a civilized hour to knock politely on this gentleman's door and request his presence at the detention center. The only reason I could come up with is that the SWAT team looks better cinematically. But without a valid plot reason for the rumpus, I mistrusted the author and eventually set the book aside.

Other potential implausibilities can occur by way of character. If it seems to the reader that a character—at least, a character functioning at optimum levels of common sense—would never do such a thing (like the teenager lost in the woods who comes to a dark house with a sign that says *Chainsaw Bill, Handyman* on it and knocks, and when no one answers, tries the door and finds it unlocked and goes inside and says, "Anybody home?") then the likely outcome is, once again, a book set-aside.

Sometimes you, the author, sniff out potential implausibility as you're writing. Other times, you'll get this kind of feedback from beta readers or editors. Now the question becomes what to do about it.

RESEARCH AND JUSTIFY

If it is a *plot* problem, see if you can attack it by *research and justification*. Ask yourself what would be needed here to make the plot development plausible? Come up with a couple of potential answers, even if they are vague. Then do pointed research to see if those choices can be justified.

For example, let's say you wrote that opening SWAT chapter we just talked about. You realize it just doesn't make sense as is. How can you make it plausible?

What if the guy in the house is a notorious assassin posing as a nice, middle-class accountant? What if he's a mad bomber who may have wired this house? What if some confidential informant who is really a double agent gave the feds false information leading them to believe this guy was an immediate threat?

When would a federal agency send in a SWAT team? A little research turned up an article which stated, "Some of the factors considered in determining SWAT utilization are the potential violence of the subject, potential risk to law enforcement and the public, location of the warrant service and case requirements." Each one of these factors can be the subject of further research.

Eventually, you should be able to find something to justify the plot development.

If you can't find a slam-dunk justification, and you feel you need to keep the plot point, you can break the emergency glass and use an old Hollywood screenwriting trick: *Skate fast over thin ice.* That is, come up with something that *sounds* plausible, state it, and get out of the scene fast.

And for every scene you write, ask a key question: *Would they really?*

Would the characters, if this were "real life," act this way? Would they make these choices? Or are you, the author, pushing them to do certain things in order to move your plot?

Another way to pose this question to yourself is: are all the characters in this scene operating at maximum capacity in order to get what they want? The sci-fi author Stanley Schmidt has wisely said, "At every significant juncture in a story, consciously look at the situation from the viewpoint of every character involved – and let each of them make the best move they can from his or her own point of view."

TRY THIS:

1. Give every character in every scene an objective, even if it's only (as Vonnegut once said) to get a glass of water.
2. Pit the agendas against each other. Even a scene between two friends or allies should have some form of tension.
3. Go into the heads of each character and record, in their voice, their action plans for the scene. This material is for you, the writer.
4. See how you can render each objective on the page visually. For example, a school custodian could step in front of a door the viewpoint character wants to enter.
5. When in doubt, use dialogue: "I'm the custodian around here, and there's no way I'm letting you in!"

MY PLOT IS TOO THIN

WHAT HAPPENS if you're writing along and get close to the middle, and you seem to have run out of plot?

Or you look ahead and see 50k words yet to be written, and you sense you haven't got nearly enough material to fill in all that space?

For this, Plotman calls upon his intrepid helper: Subplot Boy!

Hi, writers! Subplot Boy here.

There are three types of subplots—personal, romantic, thematic.

A personal subplot means the character, in addition to dealing with all the problems of the main plot, also has a personal relationship that demands his attention. This is almost always a relationship that is in place before the novel begins. Many times it involves a family member or an ex-spouse or an ex-friend, someone the Lead already knows. Often there is a wound of some sort involved in that relationship, and the personal subplot issue is whether that will be healed.

A romantic subplot happens when, during the course of the main plot, the Lead character begins to fall for another character. Don't confuse this with the romance genre, books that center on the relationship between two characters. In a genre romance, the romance *is* the main plot.

Finally, there is the thematic subplot. This involves the character in a relationship that forces her to deal with a moral question. Often this subplot is carried by a character who operates as the conscience of the Lead, or at least forces the lead to deal with an inner moral lack or need to grow.

Let me give you some examples to make things clearer.

In *Lost Light* by Michael Connelly, LAPD detective Harry Bosch takes up a case he was not able to solve years earlier. In typical thriller style, Bosch discovers that the case is far more complex than he thought, leading to a deadly, organized opposition.

Connelly is a master of the police procedural, so the first fourteen chapters follow Harry as he analyzes evidence and questions witnesses.

Then at the end of chapter fifteen he mentions his ex-wife, Eleanor Wish.

> She had pierced me through and through. There were other women before and other women since but the wound she left was always there. It would not heal right. I was still bleeding and I knew I would always bleed for her. That was just the way it had to be. There is no end of things in the heart.

This is an introduction to Harry's personal subplot. It involves a previous relationship and wound that lingers from that relationship. Harry has to deal with it at some point if he's going to move on with his life in a productive way.

Eleanor is now a professional poker player living in Las Vegas. Before that she'd been a profiler for the FBI.

In the middle of the book Harry needs to get federal agents in Los Angeles to think he's in Vegas, so he calls Eleanor and asks if she'll meet him at the Las Vegas Airport, because he needs her help. She agrees.

He hasn't seen her in three years. When she asks what's going on, he tells her about the feds, and gives her his American Express and ATM cards. He asks her to use them over the next couple of days, while he rents a car and immediately drives back to Los Angeles.

Here is where the personal intrudes again into Harry's life.

> We were on an airport road where all the Rent-A-Car complexes were lined up in a row. I wanted to say something else. Something about us and about how I wanted to come back over when all of this nastiness was finished. If she wanted me to. But she pulled into the Avis lot and put her window down to tell a security man that she was just there to drop me off. The interruption ruined the flow of the conversation, if it even was a conversation. I lost my momentum and dropped any thought of saying anything further about us.

Clearly Harry is drawn to Eleanor, but knows it's probably not going to get them back together.

Harry continues his investigation for several more chapters. Then he flies back to Vegas ostensibly to pick up his credit cards, but really wants to see Eleanor again. He meets her at a Las Vegas hotel where Eleanor, because she's a high-stakes poker player, has been given a VIP room. The old flame burns again, and the two end up in each others' arms.

Back to L.A. The case continues to its conclusion. And then we get the last chapter, which is almost always where a thriller writer will place the end of the personal subplot. One scene after all the trouble is over.

Harry goes back to Vegas one more time, only this time he goes, unannounced, to where Eleanor lives.

She's surprised to see him, of course, and Harry senses there's something askew here. Eleanor then tells Harry she has something to tell him, even though she didn't want to break it to him this way.

And that's when she introduces Harry Bosch to the daughter he never knew he had. Now it's very personal, this subplot. This is what Connelly has been leading us to.

Twin skyrockets were going off inside me. One left a trail of red, the other green. They were going different ways. One anger, one warmth. One led to the heart's dark abyss, a devil's punchbowl filled with recriminations and revenge I could dip my cup fully into. The other led away from all of that. To Paradise Road. To bright, blessed days and dark, sacred nights. It led to the place where lost light came from. My lost light.

Which direction will Harry go? The little girl shyly approaches Harry.

She lets go of her mother's hand and extended hers to me. I took it and she wrapped her tiny fingers around my index finger. I shifted forward until my knees were on the floor and I was sitting back on my heels. She peeked her eyes out at me. She didn't seem scared. Just cautious. I raised my other hand and she gave me her other hand, the fingers wrapping the same way around my one.

I leaned forward and raised her tiny fists and held them against my closed eyes. In that moment I knew all the Mysteries were solved. That I was home. That I was saved.

That's how you handle a personal subplot. Give it resonance. Make it a moment readers will be blown away by.

Now let's take up the romantic subplot. And one more time, we're not talking about the main plot of a genre romance. We're talking about other genres, be it a detective novel, a mystery, a thriller, whatever the case. We have a main character and the plot gets rolling, and the obstacles are building.

Now a further complication comes along, this time in the form of another character with whom the Lead may get involved romantically.

Consider *The Hunger Games*. The main plot is one of physical life and death. Katniss Everdeen has to fight and survive physically in the Games.

In the first chapter she is hunting illegally in the woods in order to feed her family. There she meets up with Gale. He's her closest friend, but maybe more. Will Gale become a love interest? Maybe.

But then Katniss's little sister, Prim, is chosen to be a tribute for their District. Katniss steps in to take her place. Then a male tribute from the District is chosen, Peeta Mellark. Katniss has had only one interaction with him, when he showed her kindness by leaving her two loaves of bread outside a bakery. Now he has become someone whose task will be to kill or be killed, just as it is hers.

When they begin their training, there is an obvious tension. Peeta is acting nice, but Katniss wonders if it's just a ruse to put her off balance.

> A kind Peeta Mellark is far more dangerous to me than an unkind one. Kind people have a way of working their way inside me and rooting there. And I can't let Peeta do this. Not where we're going. So I decide, from this moment on, to have as little as possible to do with the baker's son.

The Games begin and there are all sorts of physical and emotional challenges for Katniss. Heading toward Act 3 of the book she encounters a wounded Peeta and takes care of him. In spite of everything, she has to recognize her emotions.

> I'm not as smooth with words as Peeta. And while I was talking, the idea of actually losing Peeta hit me again and I realized how much I don't want him to die and it's not about the sponsors. And it's not about what will happen back home. And it's not just that I don't want to be alone. It's him. I do not want to lose the boy with the bread.

Her emotions are in conflict with her goals. If she lets her guard down, she might die. And Peeta, too. But they end up as a team so they can survive against the deadly tribute Cato.

> We stand there a while, locked in an embrace, feeling each other,

the sunlight, the rustle of the leaves at our feet. Then without a word, we break apart and head for the lake.

Author Suzanne Collins doesn't need her narrator to tell us how she's feeling. The description says it all.

And this is how a romantic subplot is interacting with, and making more complicated, the main plot of physical survival.

At the end of the book Peeta and Katniss have survived, and now must act as if they are desperately in love. Katniss doesn't know what to think.

> I haven't even begun to separate out my feelings about Peeta. It's too complicated. What I did as part of the Games. As opposed to what I did out of anger at the Capitol. Or because of how it would be viewed back in District 12. Or simply because it was the only decent thing to do. Or what I did because I cared about him.

This confusion will not be resolved until the end of the trilogy, so it becomes a subplot throughout. And Gale will figure into this, too. Quite often a romantic subplot is a classic love triangle, which is an added layer of complication.

Finally, we have the thematic subplot. This is used to illuminate the deeper meaning of the plot. One of the classic ways to create this subplot is to introduce a character in the role of a mentor, or moral conscience, for the Lead. This character functions to teach or remind the Lead of their main purpose in life, not just the plot.

Think of Yoda in *Star Wars*. He is the teacher, the mentor, the guide to The Force. He says things like: "To answer power with power, the Jedi way this is not. In this war, a danger there is, of losing who we are."

And of course, there is Gandalf in the Lord of the Rings trilogy.

> "I wish it need not have happened in my time," said Frodo.
> "So do I," said Gandalf, "and so do all who live to see such

times. But that is not for them to decide. All we have to decide is what to do with the time that is given us."

Subplots expand and, when used rightly, deepen your novel.

TRY THIS:

1. Write a one-line description of a possible subplot for your novel under each category: personal, romantic, thematic.

2. Create or refine a subplot character who can carry each one.
    a. For the personal, what new or existing character can complicate the inner life of the Lead?
    b. For the romantic, how will the love interest begin to *complicate* the Lead's plot problems? "The course of true love never did run smooth." (Shakespeare, *A Midsummer Night's Dream.*)
    c. For the thematic, what character can appear to teach the Lead what he or she needs to know? How will this lesson require growth or sacrifice?

3. Even if you decide not to use one or more of these subplots, your understanding of the character and story will be deeper nonetheless.

MY PLOT ENDS WITH A THUD

THE HARDBOILED WRITER MICKEY SPILLANE, who was once the bestselling author in the world, said, "The first page sells that book," he once said. "The last page sells your next book."

True that, if you want a career. We've all read books or seen movies or binged TV series that pulled us in, only to be let down at the end. Even to the point of feeling cheated!

Don't do that.

Let's assume that you have written a sufficient ending, but something about it seems flat. Plotman suggests you consider two things: *meaning* and *resonance*.

MEANING

Meaning, or *theme*, is the what the story is *telling us* after it's over. This often makes writers nervous because of those days in English class when you had to read a novel and write an essay about the theme. That's why *Cliff's Notes* became so popular (and why so many students got marked down for plagiarism!)

Anyway, theme doesn't feel like fun to most writers. We want to write a really gripping story, and not worry about the meaning of it all.

But here's the hard truth: *every story has a meaning.* Every story carries a message, whether it's subtle, as in a Hemingway novel, or bonks us over the head, like an Ayn Rand doorstop. What both these authors had in common was a desire to say something in their books.

Other writers see themselves as entertainers, coming up with twisting, turning plots. Or mysteries. Or romances. And nothing more. Not that there's anything wrong with that. But you need to realize the story will have some kind of meaning nonetheless. Because human beings are wired to seek meaning, consciously or unconsciously.

So why not use this to your advantage? Shape the theme of your book for optimal effect. The best time to do this is when you've finished your first draft. Certainly you can have a theme in mind when you begin writing, but it's not essential. If you have characters in conflict over a life-and-death struggle, you'll eventually find the meaning trying to get out.

TRY THIS:

1. Imagine your Lead character twenty years after your story ends. (If your character is dead, you'll have to use a little imagination here. A ghost will work).
2. Now play reporter. You interview your character and ask, "Looking back, why do you think you had to go through all that? What can you teach us?" (This lesson is what is called in mythic structure "Return With the Elixir.")
3. Formulate this in a one-line lesson, e.g., "There's no place like home."

Now, raise the impact of this lesson by:

- Providing a visual or verbal moment when the lesson is expressed or embodied by the Lead.

- Going back to early in Act 1 and having the Lead *argue the opposite of the lesson.*

Earlier, I wrote about Rick in *Casablanca,* and how at the beginning of the film he says, "I stick my neck out for nobody." Then he does that very thing at the end. We hear it when he tells Ilsa, "But I've got a job to do too. Where I'm going, you can't follow. What I've got to do you can't be any part of. Ilsa, I'm no good at being noble. But it doesn't take much to see that the problems of three little people don't amount to a hill of beans in this crazy world. Someday you'll understand that."

And then we see it when Rick shoots Major Strasser so Ilsa and Laszlo can get away (sacrifice).

In *It's a Wonderful Life,* George Bailey learns the lesson, "No man is a failure if he has friends." And his best friends are right there in the town.

But in Act 1, during a flashback sequence, young George argues the opposite. He tells the girls, Violet and Mary, that he's going to go out exploring someday, and have two or three wives, and maybe a harem.

When the life lesson learned pays off, it's extra satisfying to the reader if the argument against it has been planted earlier.

RESONANCE

Resonance is that perfect last note, as in a beautiful symphony, that hangs in the air then stays with you long afterward.

In a novel, it's the perfect last lines to top off a successfully wrapped-up plot.

At the end of Stephen King's novella *Rita Hayworth and the Shawshank Redemption,* the narrator, Red, has finally been paroled after decades in prison. Adjusting to the outside is not easy. Red finds a note from his prison friend, Andy Dufresne, asking Red to join him in Mexico. It's a "fool's errand," but Red ends his story this way:

I find I am excited, so excited I can hardly hold the pencil in my trembling hand. I think it is the excitement that only a free man can feel, a free man starting a long journey whose conclusion is uncertain.

I hope Andy is down there.

I hope I can make it across the border.

I hope to see my friend and shake his hand.

I hope the Pacific is as blue as it has been in my dreams.

I hope.

That's resonance.

TRY THIS:

1. Write several last paragraphs. Read them aloud. You're going for the right *sound,* not merely the right sentiment.
2. Next, write your last page as a prose poem. It's similar to the page-long sentence exercise we discussed earlier in this book. This time, however, you're thinking like a poet. But don't worry! No one has to see your poem. And it's not going to be in your novel verbatim. What you're trying to do is coax out some words or phrases that sing, which you can then plug in and use for your last lines. A prose poem is set out in paragraphs, yet the words have the characteristics of poetry. Here's an example from the prose poem "Bath" by Amy Lowell:

I lie back and laugh, and let the green-white water, the sun-flawed beryl water, flow over me. The day is almost too bright to bear, the green water covers me from the too bright day. I will lie here awhile and play with the water and the sun spots. The sky is blue and high. A crow flaps by the window, and there is a whiff of tulips and narcissus in the air.

Capture that same feeling with your own prose-poem-last-page, and then select the words or images that create a good sound—and give readers supreme satisfaction as they close the book.

HOW DO I REVISE MY PLOT?

YOU'VE WORKED HARD and long and your first draft is finished.

Congrats! It's a great feeling, and an even better learning experience, to write a completed manuscript.

Now comes the work.

A famous bestselling author claims that he writes only one draft and then turns it in. However, popping the hood on that statement reveals he is an "edit as you go" writer, who painfully struggles through each chapter and edits the pages before moving on.

In other words, genius does not just drip from his fingertips to the keyboard. He has to work, too, just like all mortals.

Dean Koontz is another who works this way. He makes sure each page is just how he wants it before going on to write the next page.

My preferred method is to lightly edit the pages I wrote the day before—better word choices, clearing up any confusions and so on. Then get to the current day's pages. Push on this way and finish that first draft.

Then don't look at it for 4-6 weeks. During that interim, get to work on your next book or story. At least develop your next plot (please refer to the chapter "I've got no plot!").

Now it's time for the first read-through of your draft. Many writers are old school and prefer a hard copy on actual paper. But if you like to use an e-reader or tablet, just remember that the point is to create a *reading experience.* You are going to pretend that you are a reader of a new novel by a favorite author.

The author is you.

Indeed, I encourage you to make a mock up cover, complete with a blurb. As in:

Jay Essbee is at the top of his game in this unputdownable thriller! **- New York Herald Tribune**.

Now read through the book as briskly as you can. Do not pause to take detailed notes.

Put parentheses around sentences that need fixing.

If something is confusing, put a question mark in the margin.

If the narrative seems thin, put a circle in the margin, to indicate that you need to fill things out.

Put a line through words you want to cut.

The most important thing is that you don't slow down to revise whole pages. Just read through the book as fast as you comfortably can. Get the big picture of the plot, as a reader would.

Now what?

Ask some key questions. Here are a few. Come up with your own list for future use.

PLOT

- Are there points where a reader might be tempted to put the book aside?
- Does my book open with a disturbance?
- Is the story world vivid?
- How does the action of Act 1 compel the reader to read on?

- Are the stakes in Act 2 death (physical, professional, or psychological)?
- Is there conflict or tension in every scene?
- Do you establish a viewpoint character?
- If the scene is action, is the objective clear?
- If the scene is reaction, is the emotion clear?
- Is the dialogue crisp and tense?
- Is the ending satisfying? Does it answer all the story questions?
- Does the book end with "resonance"?

CHARACTERS

- Is my Lead worth following for a whole novel?
- Will readers bond to my Lead because he ...
- ... cares for someone other than himself?
- ... is funny, irreverent, or a rebel with a cause?
- ... is competent at something?
- ... is an underdog facing long odds without giving up?
- ... has a dream or desire readers can relate to?
- ... has undeserved misfortune, but doesn't whine about it?
- ... is in jeopardy or danger?

THE 2000 WORD TREATMENT

The British novelist John Braine wrote a book called *Writing the Novel* in which he advised the following approach:

First, you write your novel. You write it as fast as you comfortably can.

When you are finished, you set it aside, then read it through.

Your next task is to come up with a 2000 word or so summary of the plot. You work on this summary over several sessions, each time being willing to change plot points, deepen or add characters ... whatever you can do to make the plot stronger.

When you're finally satisfied that the 2000 word summary is killer, you begin from page one and write a second draft.

A similar bird's eye view of the plot and outline—yes, outline—can be produced in other ways.

One way is via the writing app Scrivener. When you write scenes in Scrivener, you automatically generate a digital index card for each scene. On each card you have a title for the scene (which can be a thumbnail line of what happens, as in, **Sam confronts Mabel at the Diner**) and a place to write in a short synopsis, such as:

> Sam drives like a maniac to Mort's diner to confront Mabel. As she serves a table he begins a verbal tirade. Mort comes out from behind and Sam pops him in the nose. Mort goes for a gun. Sam runs out and jumps in his car as shots are fired.

As an alternative, Scrivener also allows you to automatically import the first few paragraphs of your scene as the synopsis on the card. Since you know the scene so well—you wrote it, after all—you'll be reminded of what's happened just by reading the opening.

Or, you can cut and paste any part of the scene, like the last few lines or the middle "hot spot." I like to cut and paste the first two and last two paragraphs as a way of recalling the ingress and egress of a scene.

The idea is to create an easily scannable record of your entire first draft. You can print it out or look at it on the app.

Spend a day looking at, and thinking about, this record of your plot.

Then spend several days working up that 2000 word (more or less) summary. Think of it as what movie folk would call a *treatment*. You want to write it in such a way that it's a pitch to a studio head. Sell this thing as a movie a huge audience will want to see!

When you're satisfied with the treatment, show it to some people. Many writers use "beta readers" to read their drafts. The treatment is a less intensive, but no less important, look at your novel. Ask your betas to put on their "studio head" hats—would they pay to see this treatment developed into a movie? (On the care and feeding of beta readers, please see Appendix 1.)

Do they give you the "green light"? If not, rewrite the treatment. If so, rewrite the book!

PLOTMAN AND SUBPLOT BOY WISH YOU GOOD WRITING!

PLOTMAN HAS ANALYZED NOVELS, screenplays, short stories, and all things fictional for over a quarter of a century.

Amazingly, his costume still fits.

But whether he flies in to help a writing group, or goes about his everyday life disguised as mild-mannered novelist Jay Essbee, he is always pleased to help a fellow writer along the way. His faithful sidekick, Subplot Boy, feels the same way!

In that regard, what follows are two appendices relating to practical issues.

The first covers beta readers, a resource many writers find useful, and which Plotman recommends.

The second deals with some plot generating systems which cost you nothing but your time and imagination—both of which you should spend freely!

Plotman and Subplot Boy wish for you, from now on, the happy experience of creating stories that readers don't just like, but love—and will leave them wanting your next book ... and the one after that ...

Carpe Typem!
Seize the Keyboard!

APPENDIX 1: BETA READERS

AS STATED EARLIER in this book, many writers use beta readers to get feedback on their drafts. So a word or two on this subject is apt.

A good rule of thumb is 3-5 beta readers. They don't have to be writers. In fact, it may be better if they are not, as writers sometimes get caught up in the arcana of craft. This is not a bad thing for a critique group, but what you want are folks who like to *read*.

A good beta reader is one who will read your manuscript as if it is a book they have purchased, and be able to offer a quality reaction. A quality reaction is more than, "This was pretty good. Thanks for letting me see it!" To avoid this, give your betas a list of questions you'd like them to answer at the end of their reading. Don't overdo this. A sample list is as follows:

1. What did you think of the overall story?
2. What did you think of the main characters?
3. Did the plot grab you emotionally?
4. Were there spots where you felt the plot started to drag? Please name them and explain.
5. Anything you'd like to add that you feel would make this a stronger story?

How do you recruit beta readers? Over time. Make a master list of every friend, colleague and/or family member who might make a good beta. Solicit their interest. Send out to three or four or five, and assess their feedback. If a beta doesn't do enough for you, simply bump them from the master list and try another name the next time.

When you approach a potential beta, let them know you'd like to send a gift card for their efforts. You can send Starbucks or Barnes & Noble gift cards. (Amazon gift cards sent from the site put the recipient on an algorithmic list that may mean they cannot leave a review of your book when it comes out.)

Tell them they will get a complimentary, signed copy of the paperback when the book is published.

If you plan to use an Acknowledgements section, you can tell them they'll be included.

BACK IN THE golden age of pulp writing, there was a fellow named William Wallace Cook who was one of the most prolific writers of the early pulp era. The man was a machine—at both typing and plotting. So much so that he wrote a book called *Plotto*, which was a huge and intricate compendium of situations, character, themes, motives and so on. Each one of these items was numbered. Following the formula in the book, you could put together an almost infinite number of combinations and come up with the skeleton of a plot. It's a bit complicated but if you want to add it to your library you can, for it is available in a reprint edition from a couple of different publishers. An online search will turn it up.

Easier to use and more fun, is *The Storymatic* card box. It contains a huge number of cards, of two kinds—character and situation. By combining random cards you can spark an unlimited number of plot ideas.

Online, there is Writer Igniter (diymfa.com/writer-igniter). You shuffle the four categories—character, situation, prop, and setting—and use that combination to begin writing.

You can use a simple dictionary. I carry around a pocket dictionary and occasionally (at my local coffee establishment) open it at random and locate a noun. Whatever that noun triggers in my mind, I riff on it for a few minutes. Free writing. A plot idea or two will bubble up. (The random-word exercise also helps when you're stuck in a scene, or when you need some ideas for upcoming chapters.)

RICHARD PRATHER METHOD

Richard S. Prather was a prolific and popular paperback writer in the 1950s and 60s. His most famous creation was the private eye Shell Scott. In an interview before his death, Prather was asked how he plotted:

> There's two types of writers: the ones who plot everything first and always know where it's going, and then you have the people who sort of wing it. One isn't necessarily better than the other, but I think the people who plot in advance are more likely to produce books that hold up over the years. I plot out everything before I start writing the story's first line.
>
> The way I've always done that is to try to get a fresh idea and just keep working with it. I'd fill up about a hundred or two-hundred pages, single-spaced, with just plotting stuff. You know, ideas, characters, and bits of dialogue, actions and reactions. I'd figure out all the movements of the story from beginning to end, and then compress that into a page or two of just the highlights. I'd then cut those highlights into chapters. I'd then expand those chapter notes, winding up with a separate page or two for each chapter and put all these pages into a folder. With every book I did I'd wind up with what I call a synopsis, it's actually an outline of maybe twenty or thirty pages, with all the action cut up into like twenty chapters. That's all there before I start the first draft.

DWIGHT SWAIN METHOD

Similar to Prather, Dwight Swain, in his classic *Techniques of the Selling Writer*, recommends creating a free form document putting down any thoughts that occur. Ideas about plot, characters, theme, whatever. Just write without editing.

The next day, review and annotate the document, then keep on going.

Repeat over the course of as many days as you like. You're not doing this to create an outline. Rather, it's a repository of your best thoughts about the book you're going to write.

DAVID MORRELL METHOD

The thriller grandmaster David Morrell also starts with a free-form document, but with a twist: he talks to himself. He asks himself questions about the story he's developing. The object is to keep digging, deeper and deeper, into the *why* of what he's thinking about. In *Lessons From a Lifetime of Writing* he states:

> I keep raising questions and answering them. I don't stick to an agenda but instead roam all over the place. I pick up and set down ideas. I go away. I come back. If I seem to exhaust one direction, I have plenty of others to explore ... I keep asking who, what, when, and how, but most of all, "So what?" and "Why, why, why?" Eventually I connect the dots and discover that I have not only a plot but characters whose issues are important to me, in other words a theme.

JSB'S FICTION HELPS

Learn to write a novel they can't put down, from #1 bestselling writing teacher James Scott Bell. His complete, all-day seminar, with handouts and a free writing book is available now, at no risk to you. For info:

https://tinyurl.com/ybpdf74c

Also available: A 24-lecture series from The Great Courses called "HOW TO WRITE BEST-SELLING FICTION." Much of the same material as covered in the above program, with added lectures on traditional and self-publishing strategies, the "mental game" of writing, and avoiding common writing mistakes. For info:

https://tinyurl.com/yykerww7

Want JSB to be your interactive writing coach, for every novel you write? Your one-time purchase of the Knockout Fiction App gives you the prompts and lets you take notes, which you can save and print out if you like. Two New York Times bestselling authors use this for each book. So can you. For info:

https://hiveword.com/knockout

WRITING BOOKS BY JSB

- *Write Your Novel From the Middle*
- *Plot & Structure*
- *Super Structure*
- *Conflict & Suspense*
- *Revision & Self-Editing*
- *27 Fiction Writing Blunders - And How Not to Make Them*
- *How to Write Dazzling Dialogue*
- *Voice: The Secret Power of Great Writing*
- *How to Make a Living as a Writer*
- *How to Write Pulp Fiction*
- *Marketing For Writers Who Hate Marketing*
- *The Art of War for Writers*
- *How to Write Short Stories and Use Them to Further Your Writing Career*
- *Self-Publishing Attack!*
- *Just Write: Creating Unforgettable Fiction and a Rewarding Writing Life*
- *The Mental Game of Writing*
- *Writing Fiction for All You're Worth*
- *Fiction Attack!*
- *How to Achieve Your Goals and Dreams*
- *How to Manage the Time of Your Life*

THRILLERS BY JSB

The Mike Romeo Thriller Series

Romeo's Rules
Romeo's Way
Romeo's Hammer
Romeo's Fight

"Mike Romeo is a terrific hero. He's smart, tough as nails, and fun to hang out with. James Scott Bell is at the top of his game here. There'll be no sleeping till after the story is over." - **John Gilstrap**, New York Times bestselling author of the Jonathan Grave thriller series

The Ty Buchanan Legal Thriller Series

Try Dying
Try Darkness
Try Fear

"Part Michael Connelly and part Raymond Chandler, Bell has an excellent ear for dialogue and makes contemporary L.A. come alive. Deftly plotted, flawlessly executed, and compulsively readable. Bell takes his place among the top authors in the crowded suspense genre." - **Sheldon Siegel**, *New York Times* bestselling author

Stand Alone Thrillers

Your Son is Alive
Blind Justice
Don't Leave Me
Final Witness
Framed

Zombie Legal Thrillers

You read that right. A new genre. Part John Grisham, part Raymond Chandler—it's just that the lawyer is dead. Mallory Caine, Zombie at Law, defends the creatures no other lawyer will touch…and longs to reclaim her real life.

Pay Me In Flesh
The Year of Eating Dangerously
I Ate The Sheriff

ABOUT THE AUTHOR

 JAMES SCOTT BELL is a winner of the International Thriller Writers Award and the author of many bestselling books for writers. He studied writing with Raymond Carver at the University of California, Santa Barbara, and graduated with honors from the University of Southern California Law Center.

A former trial lawyer, Jim writes full time in his home town of Los Angeles.

For More Information
www.jamesscottbell.com

Made in the USA
San Bernardino, CA
09 May 2020